The Teacher's Guide to the Four Blocks™

The Four-Blocks™ Literacy Model

PROFESSIONAL RESOURCES

A Multimethod, Multilevel Framework for Grades 1-3

by
Patricia M. Cunningham
Dorothy P. Hall
and
Cheryl M. Sigmon

Editors
Tracy Soles
Wolfgang Hoelscher
Louise Vaughn

Illustrators
Kathryn Mitter
Pam Thayer

DEDICATION

This book is dedicated to Margaret Defee, our pilot teacher, and all the other teachers who have worked with us and have shown us that the "Four Blocks" can and does work.

We wish to acknowledge the Wake Forest University student teachers who have used these strategies under the guidance of their cooperating teachers and went on to help others learn more about the "Four Blocks."

We recognize the efforts of the teachers at Clemmons Elementary who tried our ideas year after year and shared their successes and samples with us.

We also want to thank the teachers in South Carolina and around the country who have heard us talk or read our books and have become leaders in their schools and school districts. These teachers believe, as we do, that there is no one best way to teach reading. And so, day in and day out, they try to "do it all" so that all children may learn to read and write as we enter the next millennium.

ISBN 0-88724-494-7

TABLE OF CONTENTS

Children come in a variety of sizes, shapes, and colors. They speak a variety of dialects and languages. Even at the beginning of first grade, they vary greatly in their entering literacy levels.

Children also come with a variety of personalities and learning preferences. Some children are strong visual learners and can see a word once or twice and remember it forever. Other children are better auditory learners and can easily hear and blend sounds to figure out lots of words. Some children need a lot of structure and guidance; other children are very self-directed and learn best when they can choose topics about which they want to read and write. Some children like stories and fanciful tales; others want to read and write about nonfiction—things that really happened. The Four-Blocks literacy framework was developed to meet the diverse needs of <u>all</u> these children.

2

OVERVIEW

The philosophy or mission statement of most schools acknowledges the reality of individual differences and the fact that children do not all learn in the same way, but the daily instructional program often denies that same reality. Curriculum guides often stress whatever approach to literacy is currently fashionable. When whole language instruction was in its heyday, children were supposed to be self-directed and spend lots of time in real reading and writing while teachers were supposed to provide a stimulating environment, seizing the "teachable moment." Now that phonics is hot, teachers are supposed to conduct very structured, teacher-directed lessons, making sure that every child masters every sound before moving on!

The Four-Blocks framework was developed by teachers who believe that to be successful in teaching *all* children to read and write, we have to do it *all*! Doing it all means incorporating daily the different approaches to beginning reading.

The Four Blocks—Guided Reading, Self-Selected Reading, Writing, and Working with Words—represent four different approaches to teaching children to read. Daily instruction in all Four Blocks provides numerous and varied opportunities for all children to learn to read and write. Doing all Four Blocks acknowledges that children do not all learn in the same way and provides substantial instruction to support whatever learning personality a child has.

The other big difference between children—their different literacy levels—is approached by using a variety of formats to make each block as multilevel as possible, providing additional support for children who struggle and additional challenges for children who catch on quickly.

The Four-Blocks framework was developed in 1989-90 in one first-grade classroom (Cunningham, Hall & Defee, 1991). In the 1990-91 school year, 16 first-grade teachers in four schools used the framework, making modifications to suit a variety of different school populations, including a Title 1 school (Hall, Prevatte & Cunningham, 1995). Since 1991, the framework has been used in numerous first-, second-, and third-grade classrooms where children struggle with reading and writing (Cunningham, Hall & Defee, 1998).

SAMPLE DAY IN A FOUR-BLOCKS CLASSROOM

The remaining chapters of this book will explore each block in detail, explaining how the blocks change as the year progresses, how the blocks are different at different grade levels, and how each block is multilevel. Because all the parts of this puzzle are essential to achieving the greatest success with the framework, we want to try to simulate for you a visit to a Four-Blocks classroom. The following is a description of how one Monday in a Four-Blocks primary classroom might look. Depending on each school's schedule, the times and order of the blocks may be different.

Opening

The children enter and prepare for the day. When they have their gear stowed, they gather around the teacher. They share things that have happened to them over the weekend and talk about the events planned for the day.

Next, the teacher shows them several new informational books about animals. She picks up three or four books and shows a few pages of each. She reminds the children that each time they start a new science or social studies unit, she gathers books from both the school and the public library and puts them in a special tray or in book baskets. The children are anxious to look at the books, but it is time to get on with other things. They know, however, that this tray of books will be waiting for them during Self-Selected Reading time.

The Guided Reading Block

In this classroom, the morning begins with the Guided Reading Block. On some days, the class does a shared reading of a big book. The teacher reads the book first and then the children join in on subsequent rereadings. On other days, the teacher guides the children in the reading of selections from basal readers, literature collections, or trade books of which there are multiple copies. For today's lesson, the teacher has chosen *Spiders* by Gail Gibbons (Holiday House, 1993). As often as possible, the teacher tries to find reading material that ties in to the children's science or social studies unit. *Spiders* is perfect for their current animals unit.

This school has multiple copies of books which teachers can check out. Many of the books were selected to connect with grade-level units and themes. There are 15 copies of *Spiders*—enough for children to share as they read with partners. They are going to spend three of their Guided Reading days this week with *Spiders* and read an easier book on

A spider has four pairs of legs.

The spider has two body parts.

animals on Thursday and Friday. The teacher has chosen a good stopping point about halfway through *Spiders* and has attached a paper clip and an index card to the last page for today's reading in all copies of the book.

The teacher has assigned partners, making sure that each child who needs help has a partner who is able and willing to provide support. As she calls each pair of students to the reading area, she hands them a book and tells them that they may look at the pictures but not to remove or go beyond the paper clip! Since the teacher often clips pages to show how far students may read and encourages them to look at pictures as they are waiting for everyone to assemble, the children know just what to do.

Picture Walk

Once the class is assembled, **the teacher leads the children in a "picture walk."** The class looks at the book cover, identifying the title, *Spiders*, and the author, Gail Gibbons. The class talks about the cover picture—a large web with many different kinds of spiders. Then, they talk about each page, naming all the things they see and reading the labels that accompany some pictures. On one page, the word **arachnid** appears with its phonetic respelling—**uh-RACK-nid**. The teacher pronounces the word and has the children pronounce it with her, pointing to each part in the respelling as they say it. On the next page, students get lots of practice with phonetic respelling as they pronounce **abdomen (AB-do-men)**, **cephalothorax (sef-ah-lo-THOR-ax)**, and other spider body parts.

The children moan when they get to the page with the paper clip and index card. "I want to read it all!" several complain. The teacher expresses sympathy but reminds them that they only have 30 minutes each day for Guided Reading and that they will read the rest of the book tomorrow.

The teacher asks students what they think the index card is for and, without hesitation, they explain. Looking at a piece of chart paper which the teacher has labeled, "New Things We Learned about Spiders While Reading with Our Partners," the children know that **they should use the index card to write down a few new things they learned if they finish reading before the time is up**. The teacher reminds them that some partners will finish before others and that they should use extra time to take notes about what they want to add to the chart.

Partner Reading

The teacher sets the timer for 12 minutes and the partners quickly go to their places and start reading. **As the partners read, the teacher circulates, stopping for a minute or two with each pair of students.** She listens to their reading and discussion and makes a few notes to add later to some of the children's anecdotal records. She compliments their reading and their cooperation, especially when she notices one partner helping the other to figure out words rather than just telling the word. She also expresses her pleasure with how "grown up" they are when she sees them using their index cards to take notes.

When the timer sounds at the end of 12 minutes, the children begin to gather together. One set of partners has not quite finished reading, but the teacher asks them to join the group and finish reading quietly as the group begins suggesting things to be added to the list of spider facts. They make a long list and are amazed at what they have learned, even though they already knew a lot about spiders.

The students hand their books back to the teacher, who assures them that they will finish reading on Tuesday and add many more spider facts to the list.

New Things We Learned about Spiders While Reading with Our Partners:

1. Most spiders don't hurt people.
2. There are over 30,000 different kinds of spiders.
3. A spider has an exoskeleton which it sheds.
4. Some spiders are as big as dinner plates.
5. Spider mothers don't stay with their babies. Some take care of themselves as babies.
6. Spiders were around before dinosaurs!

30 min.

The Working with Words Block

Next on the schedule is the Working with Words Block. **Activities in this block are designed to help children achieve two critical goals:**

- **In order to read and write independently, children must learn to automatically recognize and spell the high-frequency words that occur in almost everything they read and write.**

- **Children must also learn to look for patterns in words so that they can decode and spell the less-frequent words they have not been taught.**

To accomplish these two goals, the teacher depends on a daily Word Wall activity along with a second activity, which varies, designed to help the children become better decoders and spellers (Cunningham, 1995).

Word Walls

The children are seated at their desks, and, since today is Monday, they are eager to see what five new words will be added to the Word Wall. The teacher looks at Roberto, who just arrived in her classroom last Wednesday, and realizes that he does not know what the purpose of the Word Wall is. She decides to use this opportunity to remind all the children about the importance of the words selected for the Word Wall.

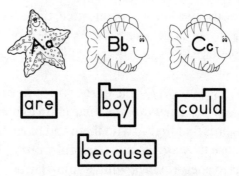

Review

The teacher begins by directing the children's attention to the Word Wall. She then asks someone to explain to Roberto how many words are added each Monday and how she decides what words to add. The children explain that **five words are added to the Word Wall each week, and these are the most important words.** When asked to explain what "most important" means, the children explain, "You use them all the time," "You can't read and write without them," and, "A lot of these words aren't always spelled the way they should be, so when you want to write one of the Word Wall words, you look up there to remember how to spell it instead of trying to figure it out."

"Why are the words arranged according to their first letter?" the teacher asks.

"To make it easier to find them. When you need the word, you just think of how it begins and then you can find it faster."

"Why are the words different colors?" the teacher asks.

"It helps you to remember those words that almost look alike—**went** is pink and **want** is green, and you can find **want** more quickly if you look for the green one under the **w**."

Adding New Words

Satisfied that the children understand why learning to read and write these words is so important, and that they know how to find the words when they need to write them, the teacher goes on to show the children the five new words that she will add today. She reminds the children of the selections they read last week during the Guided Reading time and points out that she introduced many new words as they read these selections.

She says, "It was hard to choose only five words this week, but I chose words that you see often in books, and that I think you all need when you write."

She then adds five words—**after**, **nice**, **them**, **school**, and **where**—to the wall. After adding them, she attaches gold stars to the words **nice** and **school** and underlines the spelling patterns *ice* and *ool*.

"Who can explain why some of the words have gold stars?" she asks, remembering that the class has a new student. One child explains that gold-starred words have lots of other words that rhyme with them and have the same spelling pattern. "They have stars because they are the most helpful words when you are writing. If the word you are trying to spell rhymes with a gold-starred word, you can use that spelling pattern."

The teacher demonstrates correct letter formation and has the children clap, say, and write the words on half sheets of handwriting paper. The teacher gives clues to the five new words.

Here is her first clue: "The first word I want you to practice is our new **th** word. Who can tell what it is?"

The children respond, "**them**."

The teacher then points to **them** and has students clap rhythmically and chant the letters three times: "**t-h-e-m**, **t-h-e-m**, **t-h-e-m**—**them**!" After clapping and chanting the word, students write it on their handwriting papers. The teacher demonstrates how to write the word, and the children follow her example.

She continues to ask students to identify, clap, and chant in this manner for the other four new words. After students have written all five words, she and the children check that all the letters are there and formed correctly by tracing around the shapes of the words with red pens.

The teacher finishes the Word Wall activity by reminding the children that when five new words are added, they practice only those five new words for a few days.

(On days when "old" Word Wall words are being practiced, the procedure is for the teacher to call out any five words and have the children clap them and then write them. Next, they check the words for correct spelling and handwriting by tracing around the word as the teacher traces around the same word on the board or overhead.)

Each week, as new words are added to the Word Wall, the teacher duplicates a new take-home Word Wall sheet for students to use when writing or doing other homework and passes the sheets out to the students at the end of the day.

 ## Making Words

Next, the children go into the second activity in the Working with Words Block. Today, they are *Making Words*. (On other days, the activity might be *Guess the Covered Word, Using Words You Know, Word Sorts and Hunts, Rounding Up the Rhymes, Reading/Writing Rhymes,* or another activity designed to help children learn how to decode words. See the Working with Words chapter for information on these activities.)

For this lesson, each child is given five consonant cards, **b**, **b**, **g**, **n**, **s**, and two vowel cards, **i** and **o**. In the pocket chart at the front of the room, the teacher has placed large cards with the same seven letters. The teacher's cards, like the small letter cards used by the children, have the uppercase letter on one side and the lowercase letter on the other side. The consonant letters are written in black and the two vowels are in red on both the large and small cards.

Make Step

The teacher begins by making sure that each child has all the letters that are needed. "What two vowels will we use to make words today?" she asks. The children hold up the red **i** and **o** and respond appropriately. Then, the children name the consonants.

The teacher then writes the numeral *2* on the board and says, "The first two-letter word I want you to make today is a word that you already know—**in**."

She sends someone who has quickly spelled **in** to the pocket chart to make it with the big letters and to put an index card that has the word **in** written on it in the chart. The class then makes another two-letter word, **go**, using the same procedure.

Next, the teacher writes a *3* on the board: "Add just one letter to **go** to make the three-letter word **gob**. I'm always telling you that you don't need a whole **gob** of paste." She chooses a child who has added the **b** at the end of the word to go to the pocket chart.

The lesson continues with children making words with their individual letter cards, followed by a child going to the pocket chart to make the word and put the index card word in the pocket chart. The teacher does not wait for everyone to make the word before sending someone to the pocket chart, and some children are still making the word as it is being made with the pocket chart letters. Before moving to make another word, the teacher reminds children to fix their letters to match the word made in the pocket chart.

Directed by the teacher, the children change **gob** to **Bob** and then **sob**. Then, they make **bin** and change it to **sin**.

The teacher writes a *4* on the board and asks students to add a letter to **sin** to spell **sing**. Next, they do an "abracadabra," making **sign** out of **sing** by just changing where they put the letters. They make two more four-letter words, **song** and **snob**.

The teacher writes a *5* and they make one five-letter word, **bingo**.

"I don't have any six-letter words for you today," she says. "So I am coming around to see who has the secret word. Today is one of those days when there are two secret words, but they're both hard words. I might get to make the secret words today, but I haven't stumped you in a very long time."

The teacher explains that a "secret word" is a word that uses all the letters they are working with in today's lesson. She gives the children a minute to think. Several children have figured out that they can spell **sobbing**. She sends one of them to make **sobbing** with the big letters and put the index card word **sobbing** in the pocket chart.

"I have another secret word here, and I bet you can figure it out if you think about an author who writes great informational books—the kind of books that give a lot of interesting facts about a topic."

As she is finishing her sentence, many children realize that they can spell **Gibbons**, the last name of the author of the *Spiders* book they have just read. The teacher selects a student to come up and spell **Gibbons** in the pocket chart.

She finishes the *Making Words* part of the lesson by having all the children make the word **Gibbons**, being sure to use the capital side of their **G** cards, and checking their spelling with the pocket chart and the *Spiders* book cover.

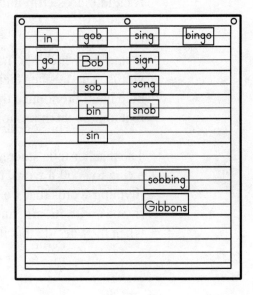

Sort Step

After making the words, it is time to sort for patterns and then use those patterns to read and spell a few new words. The teacher has the children read aloud all the words they have made, which are now displayed in the pocket chart:

First, she asks them to find the two related words. The children know that related words have the same root word and quickly pull out **sob** and **sobbing**. She helps them notice that since the word ends in **b**, you double the **b** and then add **ing**.

Then, she has the children pull out the words that rhyme and put them together in the pocket chart:

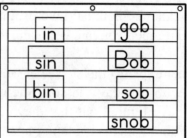

Transfer Step

The final step of every _Making Words_ lesson is the transfer step. Once the rhymes are sorted, the teacher shows the children an index card on which the new word **chin** is written.

The teacher asks, **"What if you were reading and came to this word and didn't know it?** Don't say this word even if you know it. Who can go and **put this word with the rhyming words that will help you figure it out**?"

A child places **chin** under the other **i-n** words and all the children pronounce **chin**.

Next, the teacher says, "I have a tricky word for you to figure out." She shows them a card on which she has written **knob**. A child places **knob** under the other **o-b** words. The teacher then asks students if they know any other **k-n** words that will help them pronounce this word. Many children know the word **know** and they use that to help them pronounce **knob**.

The teacher tells students, "Thinking of words that rhyme helps you when you are trying to spell a word, too. If I was writing and wanted to write **spin**, which of the rhyming words that we made today would help me?" The children decide that **spin** rhymes with **in**, **sin**, and **bin**, and they are able to spell **spin**. Then, they spell **job** when they decide that it rhymes with **gob**, **sob**, **Bob**, and **snob**.

Homework Sheet

Finally, the teacher shows students their *Making Words* homework sheet (but does not distribute it until the end of the day). The letters **i**, **o**, **b**, **b**, **g**, **n**, and **s** are in boxes along the top and there are larger boxes below for children to write words. (A blank reproducible *Making Words* homework sheet can be found on page 206.)

The children always enjoy their *Making Words* homework sheet. They cut the letters apart and then fill the boxes with words they can make, including the ones made in class and others they think of. The teacher reminds students, "When you show this to someone at your house, tell them that there are two secret words and you will probably have to tell them at least one of them. Be sure to write the capitals on the back of each letter because you can't make our secret word author's name without a capital **G**." Parents and older siblings often get involved with this activity and the students, because they made the secret word in class that day, are always "smarter" than anyone else. They enjoy stumping their often "competitive" families!

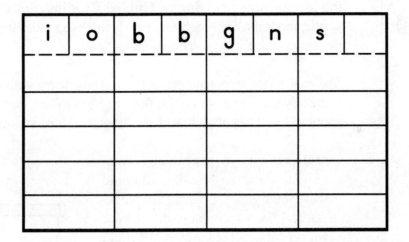

Break/Snack

Math

WRITING

The Writing Block

Mini-Lesson

The Writing Block always begins with a mini-lesson. The teacher writes and thinks aloud, modeling the way she thinks while writing. She writes about a variety of topics and in a variety of formats. Sometimes she connects her writing to what was read during Guided Reading. Since the children were so enthusiastic about the *Spiders* book, she decides to model for them how to use the information on the chart to write about spiders.

She goes to the overhead projector and sits down with a pen in hand. The children settle down in chairs or on the floor in front of her, eager to see what she will write about today. **They watch and listen as she thinks aloud about what to write:**

"I always have so many things I want to write about on Mondays...I could write about going shopping this weekend and finding my car with a flat tire when I came out of the store!...I could write about the funny movie I watched on TV...I could write a funny story about a spider...but, I think I'd rather write about some of the interesting things I learned this morning about spiders."

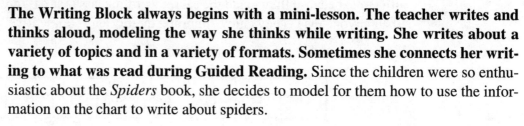

As she writes, **the teacher models for students how she might invent-spell some words.** (Earlier in the year, she told the children that she used to love to write when she was their age and that she would write all kinds of things. She wrote stories and kept a diary and was always making lists. She pretended that she was a great writer and wrote wonderful books for children to read. She explained that when she was their age, she couldn't spell all the words she needed so she just put in all the letters she could hear for the big words.) **She begins writing and spells most words correctly. Once or twice, she glances up at the Word Wall and comments, "I can spell *because* because it is on the Word Wall." She also looks at the chart and finds spellings for words like *arachnids* and *cephalothorax* from it. She stretches out the word *frightening*, spelling it f-r-i-t-n-i-n-g. She comments that she knows this probably isn't right but it will help her remember her idea. She reminds students that if she were to publish this story, she would get help with spelling the word then. She omits one ending punctuation mark and fails to capitalize one word.**

When she finishes writing, she says, "Now, I will read what I wrote to make sure that it makes sense and that it says what I want it to say." She reads aloud as the children watch and listen. As soon as she finishes reading, the children raise their hands and volunteer to be editors. She gives one boy a different color marker to go to the overhead and lead the class in helping her edit her writing. **Each editing convention the children have learned so far is covered, and the class checks her draft for these features.** The students volunteer to fix what needs fixing. Possible misspelled words are circled. Capitals and punctuation marks are added. The boy who is editing marks any changes and inserts like a pro! So far, the class has learned five editing conventions. **They read the teacher's short paragraph and put a check mark on the bottom of the page as they check these five criteria:**

1. Every sentence makes sense.

2. Every sentence begins with a capital letter.

3. Every sentence ends with a punctuation mark.

4. Names of people and places have capital letters.

5. Words that might be misspelled are circled.

Children Write

The writing mini-lesson takes approximately ten minutes, including the editing. Children are then dismissed from the big group to do their own writing. They are at various stages of the writing process. Five children are at the art table, illustrating their books. When asked why they are allowed to make books, they proudly explain that they had to write three to five pieces first. Then, they each picked the best one and read it to a friend or the teacher, who gave them ideas for revising it to make it even better. Finally, they went to the teacher for help in preparing to publish.

One child is meeting with the teacher to get help with the final edit of her piece. Two children are helping each other revise. The remaining children are working at their desks, in various stages of the writing process. Some children are beginning new pieces. Others are working on something they started the day before. Some children write about spiders. Other children write about things they did over the weekend. The teacher's mini-lesson and her pondering about what to write each morning always starts them thinking about what they will write. The children sometimes write about the same topic as the teacher, although the teacher neither encourages nor discourages them from choosing the same topic. (The teacher may wish to turn off the overhead projector or remove her writing sample before the children begin writing so they will not be tempted to copy what she has written.) Many children can be seen glancing up at the Word Wall or other places in the room when they realize that a word they are trying to spell is there.

Author's Chair

The classroom is a busy place for 15-20 minutes. Then, at a signal from the teacher, the children once again gather and the Monday children line up for "Author's Chair!" (Each child is designated by a day of the week; on his day, he shares his writing with the rest of the class.) The first child reads a few sentences of a piece that was started today. He calls on various children who tell him that they like the topic (dinosaurs) and give him ideas for what he might like to include in the piece. One child suggests a dinosaur book that he may want to read.

The second child reads a completed piece. She calls on the other children who tell her that they liked the way she stayed on the topic (her new baby sister) and ask her questions ("What's her name?" "Does she cry all night?" "Is this the only sister you've got?").

One child has written an informational piece about spiders. Another child is writing a story about spiders. Demetrius is the only Monday child who has published a book since last Monday and he proudly reads his book, entitled *The Carolina Panthers*. The sharing takes approximately ten minutes for a total of 35-40 minutes of Author's Chair.

Lunch/Recess

Science or Social Studies Unit

Special (Art, Music, P. E., etc.) or Science/Social Studies Continues

The Self-Selected Reading Block

Teacher Read-Aloud

Each day, the teacher begins this block by reading aloud to the children for 5-10 minutes. Today, she reads them an article about spiders from a children's magazine. (Teachers should also read aloud at other times during the day, if possible.)

Independent Reading

After the teacher reads to them, the children do their own reading. They choose the books they want to read from a wide variety of books available, including the new animal books the teacher showed them this morning.

Conferencing

As the class reads, the teacher conferences with the Monday children. Each child brings a book he has selected and reads a few pages from that book. The teacher makes anecdotal notes about what the Monday children are reading and about how well they are reading. She notes their use of picture clues, attempts to figure out unknown words, fluency, self-correction, and other reading behaviors. She also asks them what they like about the books they are reading and sometimes suggests other books they might like.

Reader's Chair

Each day, the Self-Selected Reading Block ends with a few children in the "Reader's Chair." They tell about what they have read that day, sometimes sharing their favorite part of the book and telling why they think other children would like this book. The children scheduled to share today are all enthusiastic about the new animal books.

15 min.

Daily Summary and School-Home Connection

Depending on whether they are walkers, car riders, or bus riders, the children leave the classroom in the afternoon between 3:00 and 3:10. This teacher always ends the day with centers. **Children spend between 30 and 40 minutes each day (depending on when they leave) pursuing their own interests in a variety of centers. Because the teacher wants to "wrap up the day" with all the children and they leave on a staggered schedule, she does the wrap-up before center time.** This way, all the children have their materials packed up and know what do for homework, and they can leave as they are called.

During the wrap-up, as the children prepare to go home, the teacher helps them talk about what they learned today so that they can discuss it at home. Many children come from homes in which English is not the primary language, and it is especially important to promote as much home/school talk as possible.

The teacher distributes the *Making Words* homework sheets and reminds students to bring them back tomorrow so she can see what other words could be made from those letters.

Next, the students identify the five new words added to the Word Wall today on their take-home Word Walls. The students may want to circle or mark the five new words on their sheets.

The teacher also reminds students to tell their families what they wrote about during their writing time and what they read during Self-Selected Reading. She reminds the Tuesday children that tomorrow is their day to do everything special and that they should decide which book they want to share during their conference time tomorrow. Finally, the teacher reminds students about their math homework and to do their 15 minutes of at-home reading.

30 min.

Centers

Now, the teacher allows the children to select their centers. Some centers—art, computer, listening, writing, magazines, big books, math manipulatives, puzzles, board games—are available all year, although new materials are added periodically. Other centers are related to holidays and the units/themes the children are studying. **There is also a teacher center in which the teacher works for brief periods with individuals or small groups.**

Each center has a specified number of tickets. Children who are going to spend part of their time in the teacher center get to choose their other center first. This makes up for the fact that they use some of their center time during their brief meeting with the teacher. Next, the Monday children choose a ticket, followed by the Tuesday children, Wednesday children, and so on (tomorrow, the Tuesday children will choose first, after those who must visit the teacher center).

The teacher makes sure all the children are where they belong and then meets with small groups and individual children in the teacher center. She chooses these children for a variety of reasons:

- If a child has been absent for several days, the teacher often takes some individual time to help that child catch up.

- If a child has had an unusually difficult day or seemed distracted or withdrawn, she often takes a few minutes with that child to talk through the problems the child is experiencing.

- She sometimes meets with a small group that needs extra help with math, and often meets with some of her struggling readers to read some easy books and to coach them to use their word and comprehension strategies.

- On some days, if she is falling behind in the publishing process, she works with a few children to get a piece ready to publish.

While the teacher does most of her assessment by observing and recording children's actual reading, writing, and working with words, she also does running records to determine children's progress. She does running records more often with her struggling readers, and center time provides the perfect opportunity to do these.

The center time at the end of the day makes for a more balanced instructional program for all the children. **During most of the rest of the day, the children pursue the teacher's agenda, but in centers they learn by pursuing their own interests.** It also provides some balance in the way the teacher spends her time, allowing some time each day for one-on-one and very small group instruction.

For many of us, being read to as a child or reading a little before "lights out" was a familiar bedtime ritual. In homes today, television, computers, and video games have all but replaced this reading event. How much a child reads is the best indicator of how well that child reads—the best readers read a lot. Children who don't like to read simply haven't found the right book yet!

Children who have been read to regularly and who have time each day to read books will become readers. Readers are not just people who CAN read—readers are people who DO read! In years gone by, the Self-Selected Reading Block was usually done at home! For most children, this is no longer true. Our Self-Selected Reading Block ensures that all children experience daily read-alouds and time for reading books of their choice and on their own level.

THE SELF-SELECTED READING BLOCK

30 min.

Goals:

- **Share different kinds of literature through teacher read-aloud.**
- **Encourage children's reading interests.**
- **Provide instructional-level materials.**
- **Build intrinsic motivation.**

Historically called individualized reading or personalized reading (Veatch, 1959), Self-Selected Reading time is now often labeled Reader's Workshop (Routman, 1995). Regardless of what it is called, **Self-Selected Reading is that part of a balanced literacy program during which children get to choose what they want to read and to what parts of their reading they want to respond. Opportunities are provided for children to share and respond to what is read. Teachers hold individual conferences with children about their books.**

The Self-Selected Reading Block includes the following:

- **Teacher read-alouds.** The teacher begins the block by reading to the children from a wide range of literature.

- **Children reading "on their own level" from a variety of books.** Books in the classroom library include books related to themes the class is studying, easy and hard library books, old favorites, easy predictable books, etc. Every effort is made to have the widest possible range of genres and levels available.

- **Teacher conferencing with students.** While the children read, the teacher conferences with several children each day.

- **Opportunities for children to share what they are reading with their peers.**

30 min.

SELF-SELECTED READING

Because all children are read to from a variety of books and have time to read books they have selected on their own, Self-Selected Reading probably varies less across classrooms, grade-levels, and time of the year than any other block. Still, there are some differences you would notice if you came to visit during this block.

5-10 min.

Teacher Read-Aloud

Becoming a Nation of Readers (Anderson, Hiebert, Scott & Wilkinson, 1985) asserts that **reading aloud to children is the single most important activity for creating the motivation and background knowledge essential for success in reading. It is hard to imagine any other activity that is so simple to do yet has so many benefits, such as:**

- Building children's motivation for becoming lifelong readers.

- Increasing background knowledge on many topics.

- Developing listening and speaking vocabularies. This is important for all children, but is critical for children who are learning English as a second language.

- Teaching about story elements and structure. Stories have characters, settings, and problems or goals which are resolved in some way.

- Getting ideas for writing from books they have heard. They see how authors create many different kinds of books.

- Providing vicarious experiences for children with limited firsthand experience. Books can take you to a big city, to a desert, back in time to the days of the pioneers, and forward in time to colonies on the moon. Multicultural books can help children learn to appreciate different people and places.

Variations in Read-Aloud Material

Variety—which is important in all teaching activities—is particularly important in the choice of books read aloud to children. When teachers are asked to list several books they have read aloud in the last month, some of the most popular titles include *Swimmy* by Leo Lionni (Pantheon, 1963), *Make Way for Ducklings* by Robert McCloskey (Puffin, 1976), *Strega Nona* by Tomie dePaola (Simon & Schuster, 1975), *Ira Sleeps Over*

by Bernard Waber (Houghton Mifflin Co., 1979), and *The Mouse and the Motorcycle* by Beverly Cleary (Dell Publ., 1965). Seldom has anyone included an informational book about animals, an informational book about sports, an informational book about another country, a biography, a mystery, or poetry. Often, the only books teachers report reading to children are fiction—stories and chapter books. A nationwide survey of 537 elementary classroom teachers (Hoffman, Rose & Battle, 1993) found that **not one of the most frequently listed read-aloud titles at any grade level was a nonfiction book**.

This predominance of fiction over nonfiction for teacher read-aloud choices makes sense if you consider that, until very recently, most of the wonderful children's books were stories. **In the last decade, however, many of the best new children's books have been nonfiction titles.** Authors such as Gail Gibbons, Joanna Cole, and Seymour Simon have created collections of truly "informing" books.

Stories should be part of every teacher's read-aloud program, but not all children like stories. Many children want to learn about "real things." The world of children's books has expanded enormously in the past decade. There is something for everyone out there. We believe that **a child who does not like to read is a child who has not found the right book.** Reading aloud from a variety of books—easy books, challenging books, one-sitting books, chapter books, Dr. Seuss books, Clifford books, mysteries, biographies, rhyming books, and all kinds of informational books—will help every child realize there are books out there they can't wait to read.

Children's Books

Read-Aloud Books Recommended by Primary Teachers

Story Books

Alexander's Horrible Terrible No Good Very Bad Day by Judith Viorst (Atheneum, 1972).

Amelia Bedelia books by Peggy Parrish (Harper & Row).

Arthur books by Marc Brown (Little, Brown & Co.).

Berenstain Bear books by Stan and Jan Berenstain (Scholastic).

Best Friends by Steven Kellogg (Dial, 1986).

Clifford books by Norman Bridwell (Scholastic).

Ira Sleeps Over by Bernard Waber (Houghton Mifflin, 1972).

Mufaro's Beautiful Daughters: An African Tale by John Steptoe (Mulberry Books, 1993).

We're Going on a Bear Hunt retold by Michael Rosen (McElderry Books, 1989).

Where the Wild Things Are by Maurice Sendak (Harper & Row, 1963).

Beginning Chapter Books

The Adventures of Doctor Underpants by Dave Pilkey (Scholastic, 1997).

Amber Brown Sees Red by Paula Danziger (Scholastic, 1995).

Godzilla Ate My Homework by Marcia Thornton Jones (Scholastic, 1997).

Junie B. Jones Is a Party Animal (and other Junie B. Jones books) by Barbara Park (Knopf, 1997).

Rats on My Roof by James Marshall (Puffin Chapters, 1997).

Chapter Books

Back to the Titanic! by Beatrice Gormley (Turtleback, 1994).

Charlie and the Chocolate Factory by Roald Dahl (Knopf, 1973).

Charlotte's Web by E.B. White (Harper & Row, 1953).

James and the Giant Peach by Roald Dahl (Puffin, 1996).

Ramona Quimby, Age 8 by Beverly Cleary (Morrow, 1981).

Scary/Mystery Books

Box-Car Children Mysteries by Gertrude Chandler Warner (Scholastic).

Encyclopedia Brown Mysteries by Donald Sobol (Bantam Books).

Nate the Great series by Marjorie Sharmat (Cowan, McCann, Inc.).

There's a Nightmare in My Closet by Mercer Mayer (Dial, 1968).

There's an Alligator under My Bed by Mercer Mayer (Geoghegan, 1972).

Biography

Jackie Robinson: He Was the First by David Adler (Holiday House, 1989).

Jesse Owens: Olympic Star by David Adler (Holiday House, 1986).

Johnny Appleseed by Gini Hollard (Raintree/Steck, 1997).

Lincoln: A Photo Biography by Russell Fredman (Clarion, 1987).

Martin Luther King, Jr. by David Adler (Holiday House, 1989).

Alphabet Books

A is for Africa by Jean Carey Bond (Franklin Watts, 1969).

A My Name is Alice by Ann Bayer (Dial, 1984).

Alphabetics by Suse MacDonald (Bradbury Press, 1987).

Eating the Alphabet: Fruits and Vegetables from A-Z by Lois Ehlert (Harcourt Brace Jovanovich, 1989).

The NBA Action from A-Z by James Preller (Scholastic, 1996).

Poetry

A Light in the Attic by Shel Silverstein (Harper & Row, 1981).

Make a Joyful Sound:Poetry for Children by African-American Poets edited by Deborah Sher (Checkerboard, 1991).

Miss Mary Mack and other Children's Street Rhymes by Joanne Cole & Stephanie Calmeasor (Morrow Jr. Books, 1990).

The New Kid on the Block by Jack Prelutsky (Greenwillow Books, 1984).

Where the Sidewalk Ends by Shel Silverstein (Harper & Row, 1974).

Information, Math

Alexander Who Used to Be Rich Last Sunday by Judith Viorst (Aladdin Books, 1988).

Each Orange Has Eight Slices by Paul Giganti, Jr. (Greenwillow, 1992).

Eating Fractions by Bruce McMillan (Scholastic, 1991).

From One to One Hundred by Teri Sloan (Dutton, 1991).

How Much Is a Million? by David Schwartz (Lapthrop, 1985).

Information, Science

Dinosaurs by Gail Gibbons (Holiday House, 1987).

Everybody Needs a Rock by Baylor Byrd (Scribner, 1974).

Journey into a Black Hole by Franklyn Branley (Crowell, 1986).

The Magic School Bus series by Joanna Cole (Scholastic).

The Sun by Seymour Simon (Morrow, 1985).

Information, Social Studies

If You Sailed on the Mayflower by Ann McGovern (Four Winds Press, 1966).

If You Traveled on the Underground Railroad by Ellen Levine (Scholastic, 1985).

The Ox Cart Man by Donald Hall (Viking, 1979).

I Have a Dream by Margaret Davidson (Scholastic, 1986).

Fiction that Builds Concepts

Anno's Counting Book by Anno Mitsumasa (Crowell, 1977).

Chicken Soup with Rice by Maurice Sendak (Harper & Row, 1962).

Exactly the Opposite by Tana Hoban (Greenwillow, 1978).

The Jolly Postman or Other People's Letters by Janet & Allen Ahlberg (Little Brown & Co., 1986).

Classics
Goodnight Moon by Margaret Wise Brown (Harper, 1947).
Little Red Riding Hood retold by John Goodale (McElderry, 1988).
Make Way for Ducklings by Robert McCloskey (Viking, 1941).
Winnie the Pooh books by A.A. Milne (E.P. Dutton, 1954)
Charlotte's Web by E. B. White (Scholastic, 1952)

Favorite Authors

Judy Blume	Leo Lionni
Eric Carle	Dr. Seuss
Beverly Cleary	Gail Gibbons
Tomie dePaola	Bill Martin, Jr.

15-20 min.

Children Read and Conference with the Teacher
Variations in Where Children Read
Tables with Book Crates

Perhaps the most noticeable difference between Four-Blocks classrooms would be where the children are during Self-Selected Reading. In some classrooms, the children are at their desks, and they read from crates of books which rotate from table to table. Each crate contains a wide range of levels and types of books, and children choose books from the crates on their tables. Classrooms that use the crates usually have a reserved book system. A child who is in the middle of a book from a particular crate (which will be moving on) can reserve that book by putting a special reserved book marker in it. Children love having favorite books on reserve for themselves!

Centers

In other classrooms, you will see children reading at a variety of centers. In addition to a reading center, many classrooms have centers such as:

- a big book center

- a magazine center

- a class-authored book center

- a science center which includes informational books on the current science topic

- a center full of books by a particular author being studied

- a taped-book read-along center

- sometimes even a computer center with a book on CD-ROM

At Self-Selected Reading time, children go to these centers. In some classrooms, they rotate through the centers on different days, and in other classrooms they choose the center to which they want to go.

Book Crates and Centers Combined

In still other classrooms, both the crate and the center variations are combined. On Monday, half the class reads from the rotating crates of books at their desks while the other half reads in centers. On Tuesday, this is reversed. This variation is particularly helpful in small classrooms where there are not many spaces for centers and where children would be crowded together at their tables if they were all reading there. Young children tend to "vocalize" as they read. We teach them to use "whisper voices," but it is still not a silent time! Everyone's concentration is improved when there is as much distance between children as possible.

Regardless of where the children are, classrooms with successful Self-Selected Reading time rigorously enforce the "no wandering" rule. Once you get to your spot, you stay there! In fact, in many classrooms, when children wander from their centers or do not appear to be engaging in the books there, they are sent back to their desks. After a few times, children seldom need to be sent back.

Variations in How Children Read

Another variation you will see during the Self-Selected Reading Block has to do with how children read books. **A commonly-observed phenomenon in homes where four-year-olds have books and someone to read those books to them is what we call "pretend reading."** Young children want to do all the things that the big people can do. They pretend to cook, to drive, to be the mommy or the daddy, and they pretend they can read. They do this pretend reading to a younger child or to a stuffed animal, and they do it with a book which they have insisted on having read to them over and over until they can "read" it! (In fact, this insistence on having a favorite book read hundreds of time is probably motivated by their desire to learn to read!)

Another way young children read books is by "reading the pictures." This is usually done with an informational picture book on a topic of great interest to the child. The parent and the child have probably looked at "the airplane book" or "the dinosaurs book" many times, spending more time talking about the pictures than actually reading the words. In fact, some of these books have wonderful pictures with lots of sophisticated text; parents may not read the text at all, they just talk with the child about the pictures.

We teach our early first graders that there are three ways to read:

- **You can "pretend read" by telling the story of a familiar storybook.**

- **You can "picture read" by looking at a book about real things with lots of pictures and talking about all the things you see in the pictures.**

- **You can read by reading all the words.**

Early in the year, we model all three types of reading, look at books, and help children decide how they might read each book:

- "*Goldilocks and the Three Bears* is a book you could pretend read because you know the story so well. Let's practice how you might pretend read it if you choose it for Self-Selected Reading time."

- "How would you read this book about the zoo? It's got lots and lots of words in tiny print, but you could read it by picture reading. Let's practice picture reading."

- "Now, here is an alphabet book. You see just one word and it goes with the picture. You can probably read this book by reading the words."

Once children know that there are three ways to read books, no child ever says, "I can't read yet!"

Teaching children that there are three ways to read—pretend reading, picture reading, and reading the words—is a variation used only in first grade. Because we provide lots of easy-reading books on many different topics, we expect second and third graders to read books by reading the words. If an individual second or third grader needs to begin at the pretend reading or picture reading level, we do this with that child during the conference, not with the entire class.

Conference Variations

Once the Self-Selected Reading Block gets up and running and children know where they are to go and how they are to read during this time, teachers usually hold individual conferences with children. **This critical conference time is how this block differs from other models of silent sustained reading or DEAR** (Drop Everything and Read).

It is important for teachers to model that they are also readers, that they enjoy personal reading, and that reading is a vital part of their everyday lives. Teachers must find other appropriate times to share what they enjoy reading, such as taking a moment during the circle time at the beginning of the day to say, "Boys and girls, when I got home yesterday, I sat down to read the newspaper and came across this funny article about a mother duck and her baby ducklings strolling down the interstate. I brought it to share with you today." Kids need to know that reading and writing are useful and enjoyable beyond the classroom. **The conference time, however, provides some of the only one-on-one, individual time afforded to students throughout the school day.**

There are several ways to hold a conference. **Some teachers go to where the children are reading and conference with them there. Other teachers sit at a table and call students over to conference with them.**

Basic Conference Procedure

First, most teachers ask each child to read a page or two from his chosen book to make sure that the child is reading "on level."

The teacher may then ask a general question or two:

- Why did you choose this book?
- Have you read any other book by this author? Which one?
- Is your book a fiction (made-up) book or nonfiction (informational) book? How can you tell?
- What do you think will happen next? Why do you say that?
- How did the author make the facts interesting in this book? Show me an example.

The teacher also encourages the student to look at reading from a writer's point of view:

- How did the author let you know that the main character was scared?
- Why was the beach a good setting for the story?
- If you had written this story, would you have chosen the same setting? Why or why not?
- Did you learn anything from this book that you can use in your own writing? If so, what?

If students have been working on a particular comprehension skill during Guided Reading, the teacher may ask questions that help the child apply these skills to the book he's chosen:

- Who are the characters?
- What is the setting?
- Was there a problem and did it get solved?
- Can you tell me what happened at the beginning, middle, and end of your story?
- What new facts did you learn from this book?
- This book has wonderful pictures of real places. Tell me about the pictures and what you learned from the pictures.
- Can you explain this chart about the parts of the animal's body to me?
- Can you read the map and explain where he traveled?

All children like to tell "what they think!" **Use open-ended questions to help them form opinions and tell about their reading preferences:**

- Do you like this book? Why or why not?

- What did you like about this book?

- What didn't you like about this book?

- What was your favorite part?

- Who was your favorite character? Why?

- Did the book have any pictures you really liked? Which one(s)?

- What was the most interesting thing you learned in this book?

- What was the funniest (saddest, most surprising, silliest, strangest) part of this book?

As the year progresses and children become fluent readers, there is more discussion and less reading aloud during the conference time. With fluent readers, reading aloud is used mostly to support the discussion.

Variations in Conference Focus

Occasionally, the teacher may want to help children anticipate the focus of the conference. In a classroom where a teacher has been stressing a certain skill or strategy during the Guided Reading or Writing Block, the teacher may say to the students, "We've been studying this week about how important the setting can be to a story. When you bring your book to share with me this week, let's talk about the setting of your book and whether it's important to the story."

She may want to remind them, "If you're reading an informational book, you probably won't have a setting because that's something writers include in telling a story, rather than when they write informational books."

Bookmarks

When students begin to read chapter books, teachers may want to give each student a few bookmarks. These are used to mark the place of a story element or of something interesting found during reading that the student may wish to discuss during the conference time. This could help save time during the conference because the students won't have to thumb through pages hunting for something. Also, in an unobtrusive way, the bookmarks could serve to remind students about the elements of story as they are reading.

A set of bookmarks can be duplicated in an array of colors for each student and kept in student reading folders or in the book baskets. Be sure to include some bookmarks that focus on enjoyment, such as a favorite part of the book, a really "neat" description, or an "I didn't know that!" discovery. Students should use only one or two bookmarks at a sitting since placing the bookmark should not become the main focus of reading. Enjoyment should always be the focus! (Sample bookmarks can be duplicated from pages 203-205.)

Conference Scheduling and Focus

Some teachers assign children specific days and then conference with them on their day, spending three or four minutes with each child. Children know that on their day, they should each bring one book to share with the teacher. They read a few pages to the teacher, discuss the book, and tell why they chose it.

Book Choices

The major purpose of the reading conference is to encourage, help and support children's independent reading. How much reading aloud is done, the types of questions asked, and the support offered by the teacher depends on the needs of each child. While letting students choose their own books is critical, teachers sometimes suggest books and authors they think children would enjoy.

If children consistently pick books that are much too easy for them, teachers may recommend more challenging books:

- "I know you like books about animals. This animal book is a little bit harder, but it has a lot of information, and you are a good reader. I think you could handle it. Why not try this book and let me know in our conference next week if it was too hard or just right, and if you liked it."

- "I bet you would enjoy reading some chapter books like the chapter book I'm reading to the class now. Here are three chapter books which lots of good readers your age like to read as their first chapter books. Do you think you might like to read one of these?"

Likewise, if children select books that are much too hard, teachers may show them how to choose books closer to their level:

- "The book you brought today is a good book, but it seems awfully hard. Here are some books that are like the book you chose, but which I think you would enjoy more. Let's try a few pages in one of these books and see if you like it and can read it better."

- Some teachers teach children the "five finger rule." If there are five words on a page that you can't decode, the book is probably too hard to read alone.

- Some children are reading chapter books at home and want to continue reading them at school and conference with the teacher about them. While lots of books are available in the classroom, children should also be encouraged to bring appropriate books from home or from the library.

Assessment

While most of the conference time is spent talking with children about books and encouraging their reading interests, **this time is occasionally used to assess how well children are progressing. If a new child moves into the classroom, the teacher might use the conference time with that child to determine his reading level. In some schools, teachers use the conference time just before report cards to take running records and get other information about how well children are progressing in reading.**

Teachers in Four-Blocks classrooms usually have a folder for each student in which they record information they learn through the conferences. Some prefer having a conference form with particular reading skills or strategies listed that they can check as having observed or not observed. Some teachers prefer strictly to make anecdotal notes about the conference, from which they can later characterize progress over several weeks. A teacher may note that "Timmy is unable to identify any of the characters in his story," "Brenda stops at unknown words and does not draw on any strategies to decode," "Tyrell was able to read aloud four pages of print in his book today!" or "Ty used context clues twice to decode unknown words." Although the anecdotal records a teacher keeps are an important part of documenting progress, the teacher must work hard at not letting the child feel that information gathering is more important than the personal book chat that the two of them are having!

Sharing Variations

It is also important that children get to share books with each other. **The sharing time usually brings closure to the Self-Selected Reading Block each day.**

In most classrooms, the Self-Selected Reading Block ends with a "reader's chair" in which one or two children each day get to do a book talk. They show a favorite book, read or tell a little about the book, and then try to "sell" this book to the rest of the class. Their selling techniques appear to be quite effective, since these books are usually quickly seen in the hands of many of their classmates. **Like adults, children like to be reading the same books their friends are reading.**

Some teachers have creative ways to encourage even the shyest of students to share to the whole class:

- **Children seem to love speaking into a microphone to talk about their books.** Inexpensive microphones, even those from dollar stores that don't really amplify the voices, seem to "bring out the ham" in kids and help them to project their voices so that everyone can hear them.

- **One clever teacher always has her sharing time in a corner of the classroom where a cardboard replica of a large TV screen is hanging from the ceiling.** Students share books or make reports from behind the screen. Everyone loves being a TV star!

- **Other teachers have "reading parties" one afternoon every two or three weeks.** Children's names are pulled from a jar, and they form groups of three or four in which everyone gets to share his favorite book. Reading parties, like other parties, often include refreshments such as popcorn or cookies. Children develop all kinds of tasty associations with books and sharing!

- **Still other teachers arrange occasional outings to allow their children to read to younger children in the school.** Each child selects a favorite book and then reads it to a younger reading buddy. Especially for the weaker readers, the teacher allows appropriate time and support for practice of the books before the students share them with others so that they are confident readers.

MAKING THE SELF-SELECTED READING BLOCK MULTILEVEL

Self-Selected Reading is, by definition, multilevel. **The component of Self-Selected Reading that makes it multilevel is the fact that children choose what they want to read.** These choices, however, can be limited by what reading materials are available and how willing and able children are to read from the available resources. **To make the Self-Selected Reading Block as multilevel as possible, collect the widest range of levels, topics, and genres of books available.** There should be chapter books in first grade and very easy books in third grade. The teacher should read aloud a variety of books—including a few chapter books in first grade and some very easy informational books in third grade.

In weekly conferences with children, the teacher should praise the reading of all the children, steer struggling readers toward easy—but interesting—books, and direct advanced readers towards challenging books. If a class has a lot of third graders who need to read easy books, the teacher can set up programs in which they read to younger children and thus have a real purpose for engaging easy books. Remember that the topic of a book is critical, and children will often read books that are too easy—or even too hard—for them if they are really interested in that topic or author. **Children should be encouraged to read on their level, but remember that this is called "Self-Selected Reading"—the main goal is to have children selecting the books that will turn them into readers.**

Kids' Comments about Self-Selected Reading:

"I like reading my Boxcar Children books."

"I enjoy Self-Selected Reading because you could read alone."

"I like Self-Selected Reading because you can pick your own book."

"I like Self-Selected Reading because there is finally some quiet time."

"I like it best because the teacher reads Junie B. Jones books to us, and then we can read any interesting books."

"My favorite block is Self-Selected Reading because I like to read by myself."

The pages at the end of this chapter will provide you with a summary and review of information. There is an example of how one week in this block might look. Finally, there is a checklist many teachers use when they begin implementing this framework.

SUMMARY OF THE
SELF-SELECTED READING BLOCK

> **The purpose of this block is to build fluency in reading, to allow students to read and enjoy text that is appropriate to their own independent reading levels, and to build confidence in students as readers.**

Total Time: 30-40 minutes

5-10 min.

Segment One: Teacher Read-Aloud

The teacher reads aloud to all students from a variety of genres, topics, and authors.

15-20 min.

Segment Two: Independent Reading and Conferencing

1. Students either move to a reading area and select a book, or choose a book or magazine from the basket at their table to read independently.

2. The teacher holds conferences with 3-5 children daily as the other children read. She keeps a conference form recording each child's individual progress, preferences, and responses.

5-10 min.

Segment Three (Optional): Sharing

1. Several students share briefly (approximately two minutes each) with the whole class what they have read.

2. If time allows, the reader answers several questions from classmates about the book. The teacher models the types of thoughtful questions children should ask.

A TYPICAL WEEK IN THE SELF-SELECTED READING BLOCK

Monday

> **Read-aloud title:** *Oh, The Places You Will Go!* by Dr. Seuss, Random House, 1990 (rhyming/fiction)

Segment 1

The teacher gathers students around her rocking chair in a carpeted area of the class-room. Since the class has begun a unit on travel and transportation, she tells the students that she wants to share a book by one of their favorite authors, Dr. Seuss, who wrote about traveling. The book connects with their theme on travel and trans-portation. The children listen attentively to the story and laugh at its funny, nonsen-sical rhymes. After reading the story, the teacher tells the students that they might see this book again in the Working with Words Block because of its wonderful rhymes.

The teacher reminds the students that she has gathered a collection of printed mate-rials—books, magazines, pamphlets, etc.—that relate to the week's theme on trans-portation. One group has the option of spending their Self-Selected Reading time in the center exploring those materials, or remaining at their desks reading materials from the book basket. She dismisses each table of students one at a time to go qui-etly to their places to read. The children that conferenced with her on Friday are allowed to go to the reading center.

Segment 2

Students make independent selections of books and settle down to read. Several students are involved in reading chapter books. Their books are in the basket at their table with a personalized bookmark holding the correct place.

The teacher has conferences with five students (three to four minutes each) about their books. She keeps a record of the progress of each student. After 20 minutes of reading/conference time, the teacher alerts students that the reading time has ended.

Segment 3 (Optional)

The children gather in a carpeted area where a cardboard TV front hangs from the ceiling at just the height appropriate to frame a child sitting on a stool. Two students "appear on TV" to share a bit about the books they're reading, and tell why they would recommend the books to others.

Tuesday

> **Read-aloud title:** *The Armadillo from Amarillo* by Lynne Cherry, Harcourt Brace & Company, 1994 (fiction)

Segment 1

The teacher gathers students around her rocking chair for the read-aloud. Once the children are settled and quiet, the teacher introduces a story which she says is similar to the one the class is reading in their Guided Reading Block. It is about an animal that travels, and it will show them different and exciting ways to go places. The traveling animal which is shown on the cover of the book is an armadillo riding on the back of an eagle. What an exciting ride that would be! The children listen quietly as the story is read and as the colorful illustrations are shared with them.

As the teacher dismisses the students to begin their independent reading time, the Monday group is invited to go to the reading center to explore the theme-related books among other books located there. The other students return to their tables to choose books from the book baskets.

Segment 2

The students read quietly while the teacher conferences with each of the four Tuesday students. The teacher has set a timer to help her pacing, and the timer sounds after 20 minutes.

Segment 3 (Optional)

Two students share on "TV" today, bringing closure to the Self-Selected Reading Block.

Wednesday

> **Read-aloud title:** *I Can't Take You Anywhere!* **by Phyllis Reynolds Naylor, Simon & Schuster, 1997 (fiction)**

Segment 1

The teacher gathers students around her at the rocking chair. She reminds them of the themes they have been studying (travel and transportation) and of the selection they have been reading during the Guided Reading Block. The dinosaurs who were traveling in that story found that there were rules and manners that made going places a lot more fun for everyone. The teacher tells students that today's story is a funny one about a little girl named Amy Audrey whose family couldn't take her anywhere. "I wonder why? What do you think? Let's read and find out!"

Segment 2

The teacher holds brief conferences with Wednesday students.

Segment 3

Two students share their books.

Thursday

> **Read-aloud title:** *Blimps* **from the True Book Series by Darlene R. Stille, Grolier, 1997 (information book)**

Segment 1

The teacher tells students that she has a book to share about a type of transportation they haven't discussed this week. She hasn't ever traveled this way, nor does she have any friends who have gotten to travel on one of these. "It's a blimp!" she says. "This book tells all kinds of neat stuff about blimps." The children listen attentively to this information book.

Segment 2

Wednesday's children go to the reading center to explore books about travel and related topics, and the other children return to their tables to choose books from the book baskets.

The teacher conferences with some Thursday children.

Segment 3 (Optional)

Two children tell about their books in the sharing center.

Friday

> **Read-aloud title:** *On the Go* by Ann Morris, Scholastic, Mulberry Books, 1994 (informational book)

Segment 1

Because her students seem to love informational books so much, the teacher shares another book of that genre on the topic of travel. This book, she points out, is illustrated with photographs instead of the drawings that are common to the books they read. The children enjoy the books and pictures.

Segment 2

The teacher conferences with Friday children as the other students read silently from book baskets or the reading center.

Segment 3 (Optional)

After the timer sounds, the teacher draws names of students who will meet together to tell each other something about their books. Each student's name is called to go to a designated place to meet with his "book talk buddy." Students take their books so that they can show what the book looks like, share how it's illustrated, and tell what they liked about it. This segment takes a few minutes longer than the usual closure time for this block, but the teacher has planned her schedule accordingly.

TEACHER'S CHECKLIST FOR SELF-SELECTED READING

In preparing and presenting my lesson in this block, I have...

_____ 1. Provided a good model of fluency in reading and attempted to motivate students through a teacher read-aloud daily. My read-aloud was clear, expressive, and enthusiastic.

_____ 2. Provided an adequate supply of books and other reading materials on various topics, of different genres, and on varied reading levels (above, below, and on grade level).

_____ 3. Made books easily accessible to children so that they will not lose time in choosing and trading books.

_____ 4. Divided the class so that I know which days I will have conferences with each child.

_____ 5. Limited the time spent on each conference to 3–5 minutes.

_____ 6. Used questions in my conferences that let children know what is important about their reading rather than emphasizing minor details.

_____ 7. Guided and encouraged children during the conference to read books on appropriate levels, while still allowing freedom of choice.

_____ 8. Promoted reading through teacher read-alouds and book talks at several appropriate times throughout the day

_____ 9. Connected read-alouds, when possible, to a subject, theme, or concept which the class has studied or will study.

In Guided Reading, teachers choose material for children to read and a purpose for reading, and then guide them to use reading strategies needed for that material and that purpose. Teachers provide guidance in a variety of whole class, small group, and partner formats.

Guided Reading is always focused on comprehension. Children learn to predict what might happen or what they might learn. They learn about the story elements of characters, setting, and plot, and they learn how to organize and compare information learned from informational text.

Guided Reading is done with all types of reading materials—big books, little versions of big books, basal readers, anthologies, magazines, multiple copies of trade books, and sections from science and social studies texts.

THE GUIDED READING BLOCK

30-40 min.

Goals:

- **Teach comprehension skills and strategies.**
- **Teach children how to read different types of literature.**
- **Develop background knowledge, oral language, and meaning vocabulary.**
- **Provide as much intructional-level reading as possible.**
- **Maintain the self-confidence and motivation of struggling readers.**

Depending on the time of year, the needs of the class, the personality of the teacher and the dictates of the school or school system, Guided Reading is carried out with the adopted basal, basal readers from previously adopted series, multiple copies of trade books, big books, and various combinations of these. **The purposes of this block are to expose children to a wide range of literature, teach comprehension strategies, and teach children how to read material that becomes increasingly harder.** When using basal readers, teachers should pick and choose activities. In the Guided Reading Block, activities are chosen that focus on comprehension.

Teachers should try to provide as much instructional-level reading during this block as possible. However, children are not reading on their levels during Guided Reading every day.

- Children who read well above grade level profit from the comprehension instruction and a balanced diet of different types of reading, but they do most of their "on-level" reading during Self-Selected Reading.

- Children who read below grade level are provided strong support when grade-level materials are being read, and they have opportunities for as much easy reading as possible. Many struggling readers, however, do most of their "on-level" reading during Self-Selected Reading and when teachers put students together in small, flexible reading groups.

If Guided Reading were the only block taught consistently in the classroom, it could not be organized as it is, but the other three blocks—Self-Selected Reading, Writing, and Working with Words—provide numerous appropriate reading and writing opportunities for above- and below-level readers.

Guided Reading lessons usually have a before-reading phase, a during-reading phase, and an after-reading phase. Depending on the text being read, the comprehension strategies being taught, and the reading levels of the children, there can be a great variety of before-, during-, and after-reading variations.

Before children read, the teacher helps them with:

- building and accessing prior knowledge
- making connections to personal experiences
- developing vocabulary essential for comprehension
- taking a "picture walk"
- making predictions
- setting purposes for their reading
- starting a graphic organizer or KWL chart

The teacher may use the following variations during reading:

- Choral reading
- Echo reading
- Shared reading
- Partner reading
- Small, flexible groups
- Three-ring circus format (alone, with partners, or with the teacher)
- Book club groups
- Everyone read to ... (ERT)
- Sticky note reading

After reading, the teacher helps the children with:

- discussing the text/literature
- connecting new knowledge to what they knew before
- following up predictions
- acting out the story
- discussing what they have learned and how they are becoming better readers by using their reading strategies
- completing the graphic organizer or KWL chart

Early in first grade, most Guided Reading time is spent in shared reading lessons with predictable big books. These books are read together in a variety of choral, echo, and other shared-reading formats. Little books based on the big books are read and reread with partners, then individually or in small groups.

As the year progresses, the shared reading of big books continues to be a part of Guided Reading, while other books, not big and not predictable, are added. These books might be part of a basal series or multiple copies of trade books. The emphasis shifts from reading together to reading with partners, in small groups, with the teacher, or individually.

Guided Reading in the primary grades usually includes several readings of each selection:

- **Instead of always reading the selection first to the children, teachers often begin Guided Reading with a "picture walk" through the book.** They lead the children to name the things in the pictures and make predictions, and they point out a few critical vocabulary words with which students might have difficulty as they read the selection.

- **Children then read the selection individually, with partners, or in small flexible groups with the teacher.** The class reconvenes, discusses the selection, and then may read it again in some other format (not round-robin, however!). Comprehension strategies are taught and practiced. Predictions made before reading are checked. Story maps and webs are completed.

- **The next reading of the selection might include a writing activity.** This writing activity is also done by some children individually, some with partners, and others in a group guided by the teacher.

- **Often the final reading is a dramatization of the selection**, with various children playing different parts as the rest of the class reads or tells the story.

As a class reads and rereads selections, the teacher uses a variety of different whole-class, small group, partner, and individual formats. Along with deciding how to read a selection, the teacher decides what can be done before and after reading to promote comprehension. The next two sections describe some of the most-commonly used before-, during-, and after-reading variations.

READING VARIATIONS

Choral Reading

Choral reading works best for poetry, refrains, and books with lots of conversation. The whole class can read, the girls and boys can alternate reading, or rows or tables can alternate. Old favorites such as "The Itsy Bitsy Spider," "Five Little Pumpkins," "Rudolph the Red-Nosed Reindeer," *Peter Cottontail,* nursery rhymes, and finger plays are naturals for choral reading. Choral reading is a wonderful way to reread books, such as *The Lion and the Mouse* retold by Cheyenne Cisco (William H. Sadler, 1997), in which two characters talk to each other. Choral reading should be used even in second and third grades because rereading provides children with the practice needed to build fluency and self-confidence.

Echo Reading

In echo reading, the teacher reads first and then the children become the echo, reading the line back to her. As students echo read, they try to match the teacher's emphasis and fluency. Echo reading is usually done one sentence at a time and is most effective when there are different voices and relatively short sentences. *Brown Bear, Brown Bear, What Do You See?* by Bill Martin, Jr. (Holt, Rinehart & Winston, 1967), *I Went Walking* by Sue Williams (Harcourt Brace, 1990), and *Hattie and the Fox* by Mem Fox (Simon and Schuster, 1968) are favorites for echo reading.

Shared Reading

One important kind of guided reading in the primary grades is shared reading with predictable big books. **Predictable books are books with repeated patterns of refrains, pictures, or rhymes. Shared reading with big books is an extension of the "lap experience" we wish all children had at home before beginning school, where the children were read to while sitting on someone's lap or snuggled close to someone.** Being read to in this way gave them an opportunity to look at pictures and print up close and to ask questions about the book. They often asked for the same book to be read over and over. In shared reading with big books, the children can see both the pictures and the print as the teacher reads. Just like at home, one reading is never enough! After one or two readings, the children chime in, having memorized the words. *Brown Bear, Brown Bear, What Do You See?* by Bill Martin, Jr. (Holt, Rinehart & Winston, 1967) and *Mrs. Wishy Washy* by Joy Cowley (Wright Group, 1998) are common books for shared reading.

Comprehension activities often include the following:

The class might "do the book," with some children assuming roles and becoming the characters as the rest of the children read the book. Little books based on the big books are read and reread with partners, then read individually or in small groups. Class books and take-home books patterned on the big book are often constructed in shared writing activities.

The big books read during Guided Reading are sometimes chosen because they fit a theme or unit the class is studying. On these days, Guided Reading time flows seamlessly into other unit-oriented activities.

Following are some examples of Shared Reading lessons.

Shared Reading for Emergent Readers

Here is an example of how you might do shared reading with emergent readers using *Moonbear's Books* by Frank Asch (Simon & Schuster, 1993).

The shared reading of *Moonbear's Books* begins as the teacher calls her children up close so they can see the book—both pictures and print.

The teacher then leads a picture walk through the book, looking at the pictures and asking, "What is this book about? I see a bear on this page . . . and books."

She turns the page and comments, "I see the bear again and another book—a big book. What do you see on the next page?" The students respond, "The bear and a little book."

The teacher continues the picture walk, talking about the bear and the books on each page. When the teacher finishes, she asks, "What do you think this book will be about?" One child says, "A bear with lots of books!"

The teacher asks the class to listen as she reads the book to find out what kind of books the bear has. She begins by showing the cover of the book, pointing to and reading the name of the book, *Moonbear's Books*, and the name of the author, Frank Asch. Next, she shows the children the title page and shares the information on that page. She is then ready to read the book.

The teacher reads each page, pointing to each word and then to the picture. When she finishes the last page with, "Moonbear loves to read," she asks the children, "What kind of books did Moonbear like?" The children name the kinds of books. They look back at several pages, talking about the opposite words **big/little**, **happy/sad**, **thick/thin**, **tall/short**, and **old/new**.

The teacher reads the book again, inviting the children to join in and share the reading with her.

Next, the teacher tells students that they are going to read the book one more time, this time watching how the pictures go with the words. They "cross check" the pages together: "There is a picture of a big book and the word before **books** begins with **b**—it must be **big**!" On the next page, there is a picture of a little book and the word before **books** begins with **l**. On each page, the teacher points to the pictures, reads the words, and then helps the children see that the words begin with the right sounds and letters. On the pages where there are thick books and thin books, the children conclude that **thick** and **thin** begin with the same letters and sound, but they can tell which word is which by looking at the pictures.

The teacher then takes out a sentence strip and turns back to the first page in the book. She writes the sentence, "Moonbear loves books." Next, she cuts the sentence into words, mixes them up, and asks, "Who can come to the front of the room and 'be' the words in this sentence?"

She gives the words to three different students. They come to the front of the class and "build the sentence" by lining themselves up in the same word order as the sentence. The teacher reads the sentence aloud, pointing to each child as she reads his word. Then, the class reads the sentence together.

The teacher then turns to the sentence at the end of the book. She writes "Moonbear loves to read" on another sentence strip, cuts it into words, and hands the words to four different children. They come up to build the sentence. The boy with the word **Moonbear** recognizes his word and gets himself in the right place at the beginning of the sentence. Another child goes to the big book, looks at the last page, figures out that she is the second word, **loves**, and takes her place. The child with the word **to** counts and steps into the right spot. The child with **read** knows the word and goes to the end of the sentence.

In Guided Reading, teachers should always focus on comprehension. The teacher asks the children to remember what kinds of books Moonbear loves to read. They remember big books, little books, thick books, thin books, old books, new books, happy books, and sad books. The teacher writes these kinds of books on sentence strips as the children name them. She then tells the children that there are two other kinds of books and turns to the pages with the tall books and short books. Then, she writes these two other kinds of books on sentence strips as well. Next, she puts all the sentence strips in a pocket chart, and she and the children read them aloud together, using the beginning letters to tell the words apart.

To focus on sequence, the teacher asks the children if the types of books written on sentence strips in the pocket chart are in the same order as they were in the book. The children don't think they are, and the teacher asks them to try to put the kinds of books in the correct sequence. They check their sequence by reading the book once again.

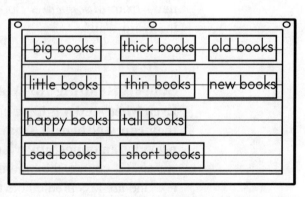

A follow-up activity for another day is to make a predictable chart patterned on the big book. The teacher models the first sentence for the predictable chart: "Moonbear likes funny books." She writes this sentence, along with her name, on the chart. The children are asked to tell what other kinds of books they think Moonbear likes. Each of their responses and their names are added to the chart.

Moonbear likes funny books.(Miss Alvarez)
Moonbear likes fancy books. (David)
Moonbear likes race car books. (Jasmine)
Moonbear likes soccer books. (Tommy)
Moonbear likes religious books. (Michelle)

When the chart is finished, the children read aloud their own sentences. As each sentence is read, the teacher writes it on a sentence strip. After all the sentences are written on sentence strips, the children are given their sentences to cut apart into words. They paste these words in order on a large sheet of paper and illustrate the sentences. The teacher staples these pages together into a class-created big book, "Moonbear Loves Books." This big book has many more pages than the original book. The children are proud of their work.

Both the original and the class-created books are available during Self-Selected Reading, and the children enjoy reading both of them over and over. The teacher chooses five words (**to**, **big**, **little**, **old**, and **new**) from *Moonbear's Books* to add to the Word Wall.

Shared Reading for More Fluent Readers
Even when students have begun to read and to develop their reading strategies, they can still benefit from the shared reading of big books. Shared reading provides an opportunity for the teacher to model a strategy as all the children watch. Of course, the big books used with more accomplished readers have more text and are less predictable than the big books used with emergent readers.

Here is an example using *The Lion and the Mouse*, retold by Cheyenne Cisco (William H. Sadler, 1997). It is a great book for helping students to develop a better understanding of characters, conversation, and quotation marks. This fable has two contrasting animals in it: a big, bossy lion and a quiet, little mouse.

The shared reading begins with a picture walk. The teacher and the children talk about what they see in the pictures. The teacher leads the children to talk about how fierce the lion looks and how he roars when he talks. Next, a quiet little mouse comes along and tries to pick a berry from a bush. As the mouse creeps closer, the lion wakes up and catches the mouse by the tail. The mouse looks like he is begging for the lion to spare his life. It looks as if the lion will eat the mouse, but on the next page the mouse is running away. Later, we see the lion caught in a rope and the mouse listening to his roars.

Before turning the page, the teacher asks, "How many of you think the mouse will help the lion? How many of you think that the mouse won't help the lion? How could the mouse help the lion?"

They turn the page and see a picture of the mouse chewing the rope and the lion walking away. The children comment that on the last pages the lion and mouse look like friends. The teacher asks, "What do you suppose they are saying to each other?"

Next, the teacher says, "Listen as I read the story of *The Lion and the Mouse*. The two characters do a lot of talking in this book. Listen to how different the lion and the mouse sound when they talk and see if you can find out what the mouse said to keep the lion from eating him."

Then the teacher reads the book. She uses a big, deep voice for the lion and a little, whisper voice for the mouse.

When she finishes reading, she asks her students, "How did the lion sound when he talked? How did the mouse sound when he talked? What did the mouse say to stop the lion from eating him?"

The children discuss the different voices of the lion and mouse and explain that the mouse kept the lion from eating him by promising to help the lion someday. The teacher and the class discuss how the mouse helped the lion and whether or not a mouse and lion could really be friends.

For the second reading of the book, the teacher turns back to the beginning of the story and comments that the first page has no quotation marks, but the second page does. She asks a child to come up and show which words are in quotation marks. Then, she reads each page and asks the children to listen to determine who is saying the words in quotation marks. After she reads the page, the children decide that the lion was talking and together they read just the words that the lion said.

For the next page, the teacher asks them if they see any quotation marks. They don't see any, so they decide no one is talking on this page. The teacher reads the page to them and they go on to the next page. Here they find some quotation marks. A child comes up and points to the words in the quotation marks. The teacher reads as the children listen for who is talking and what was said. Then, they read along with the teacher just what was said, using the appropriate loud or quiet voice. They finish the second reading of the book in this way.

For the third reading, the teacher chooses a choral reading format. She divides the class in half, into "lions" and "mice." She reads all the words not in quotation marks. The children read their animal parts, roaring or whispering. After this third reading, they discuss how the lion and mouse sounded different depending on what was happening in the story.

Since all the "mice" want to be lions, the class reads the story one more time with the children exchanging roles.

The teacher brings the shared reading activity to a close by having the children explain how quotation marks are used and how the characters change during the story.

The next day, the teacher gathers the children together and reminds them that yesterday they talked about how different the lion and mouse were. She then asks them to listen for some "opposites" as she reads the first two pages of the book. The children identify the opposites **big/little** and **quiet/noisy**. The teacher writes these on an opposites chart. They do the next two pages together and identify **yelled**, **shouted**, and **whispered**, which the teacher adds to the chart.

The teacher then explains that the children are going to read the book (little book versions of the big book) in groups of three, and they will read it three times. For the first reading, one child will be the lion, one will be the mouse, and one will be the narrator. They will switch parts for the next two readings so that each child gets to read each part. When the children finish reading, they will write down more opposites to add to the chart.

Benefits of Shared Reading

Shared reading provides opportunities for teachers to model for children how to think as they read. By using big books in which the children can see the print and pictures, teachers can focus their attention on whatever strategy is being developed. Shared reading of big books should not be confined to kindergarten and early first grade. Rather, teachers should find and use big books that help them demonstrate and "think aloud" when new comprehension strategies are being introduced.

During shared reading, there are many different things that can be learned, depending on what the children are ready to learn. Children who have had little experience with reading learn how print works, how to track print, and how the pictures and words support each other. They learn a few words and learn how noticing the letters helps you tell which word is which. For children who are further along in reading, shared reading provides an opportunity to learn many words. All children enjoy shared reading, and participating in shared reading lessons helps them build concepts, vocabulary, and comprehension strategies. There is "something for everyone" in a good shared reading lesson, and consequently, shared reading is one of the most "multilevel" formats.

Partner Reading

Children accept the fact that some of their friends are better ball players or better artists. In real life, friends often learn from and help each other. **Partner reading allows friends to help each other read, just as they help each other with other activities.**

For partner reading to be effective, children need to learn a variety of ways to do it:

- Some days are designated as "take turn" days, when the partners take turns reading the pages, helping each other as needed.

- On other days that are designated as "ask question" days, the partners read each page silently and then ask one another questions about each page before going on to the next page.

- On "sticky note" days, the partners are given self-adhesive notes to mark things they want to remember. They have a limited number of sticky notes and must decide together where to put the notes to mark what they find as most interesting, important, or confusing.

- Occasionally, the teacher declares a "you decide" day, on which the partners can decide to read together in any way they wish.

Having these different kinds of partner-reading formats provides some variety in the reading. It also ensures that children engage in both silent and oral reading.

Assigning Partners

There are a variety of ways to assign children to partners. **Generally, the teacher should pair children who work well together.** It would be ideal to pair a child who is struggling with a child who can help—and who will help "nicely." A partner who belittles a struggling reader will not provide the kind of support and confidence building that is needed.

Some teachers use stickers in different colors and shapes to designate the partners and to determine who will read first. Imagine that you have a selection that many children in your class will need support in reading. You want all the children who will need help to have a partner who will help nicely. You also want the better readers to read the first two-page spread, in which many of the names and other important vocabulary words are used.

1. Consider who you will pair with whom, pairing the most struggling readers with your most considerate and nurturing better readers.

2. Give the stronger reader in each pair a blue square and give the other child the blue circle. Continue with other colors until everyone has a sticker.

3. When it is time to read, simply have the children find partners with the same color stickers and tell the children that, today, squares read first.

4. All the partners who cooperate well, help each other, and use quiet voices get to keep their stickers!

Teacher's Role

When all the children are reading with partners, the teacher circulates through the classroom, listening to them read, helping if needed, and making anecdotal notes. These notes should be about children's reading fluency, their discussion, how they are figuring out words, and how they are helping one another. By stopping for just a minute and listening to each set of partners, teachers can monitor all the children's reading in a 12-15 minute period.

SMALL GROUP

Coaching Groups: Small, Flexible Groups

Often, the teacher meets with a small, flexible group of students to coach them as they are reading. The children in this group participate in the before- and after-reading activities with the whole class; this coaching group is how the teacher helps students apply the strategies they have been learning. When reading with the small group, the teacher should try to avoid "turn-taking." The children should read softly, but still loud enough for the teacher to hear and coach them when they need help.

Before the children start to read, remind them of the strategies they can use to figure out an unfamiliar word:

1. Put your finger on the unknown word and say all the letters.

2. Use the letters and the picture clues.

3. Try to pronounce the word by looking to see if it has a spelling pattern that you know.

4. Keep your finger on the word and read the rest of the sentence to see if what you think the word is would make sense.

5. If it doesn't make sense, go back to the word in the sentence and try to think what would make sense and would have these letters.

When a student is stumped by a word while reading, the teacher prompts the child to use these strategies by giving clues, such as:

- "Yes, this word is spelled **g-r-u-m-p**. We have a word on our Word Wall spelled **j-u-m-p**."

- "Do you see an animal in the picture that might be spelled **d-r-a-g-o-n**?"

- "What could you dig a hole with that begins with the sound **sh**?"

Once the child has figured out a word, the teacher reminds him to go back and reread the sentence to see if it sounds right.

Teachers call together coaching groups for a variety of reasons. Children who need a lot of support are included in these groups more often than accelerated readers, but these groups are <u>not</u> ability-based groups. The members of the groups change each time a coaching group is called, and the teacher should include some able readers to model good reading strategies.

INDIVIDUAL

PARTNERS

SMALL GROUP

Three–Ring Circus

On some days, the teacher may want certain children to read the selection on their own, while others read it with partners and the teacher meets with a small "coaching" group. This "three-ring circus" is not as difficult to achieve as might be expected.

1. First, explain to students that there are advantages to all three types of reading. When they are reading by themselves, they can read at their own pace and focus on their own ideas. When they are partner reading, they have the advantage of getting help when they need it, and they have someone with whom to share ideas. Explain to the students that you like to read with a small group so that you can see how they are progressing and help them apply the strategies they are learning.

2. Second, make sure the children know how to read with their partners and what kind of partner format you want them to use on this particular day.

3. Finally, you need an organizational chart so that children can quickly see how they will read the selection that day and not waste time waiting for you to get everyone in the right place. Below is a "three-ring circus chart" one teacher uses to let students know how they will be reading. On days when the teacher wants to have a three-ring circus organization, she places the children's names in the appropriate rings.

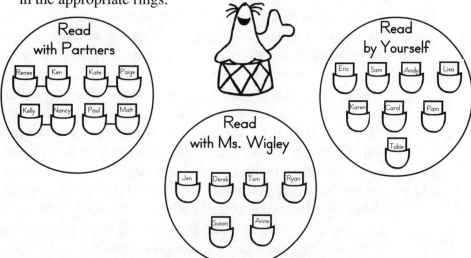

When planning a three-ring circus, consider the levels of both the children and the reading selection in deciding which method each child should use for reading. Accelerated readers often read the selection individually or with partners of similar ability. Children who need support are paired with supportive partners or assigned to the coaching group. Do not assign pairs who do not work well together, and never assign a child to read individually unless he can successfully complete the reading on his own.

SMALL
GROUP

"Book Club" Groups

For Book Club Groups, the teacher selects three or four books which are tied together by author, genre, topic, or theme. After reading aloud the first chapter or several pages of each book, or previewing the pictures with the children, the teacher has children indicate their first and second choices (and a third choice, if there are four books) for which book they would like to read.

When choosing the books for Book Club Groups, the teacher should try to include one that is easier and one that is harder. If children who are struggling list the easier book as one of their choices, they are put in the group that will read this book. If the more advanced readers list the harder book as one of their choices, they are put in that group. (Don't tell the children that some books are harder or easier!) Each time a class does Book Club Groups, the students are placed in different groups. While the reading levels and choices of children are considered when assigning, the groups all have a range of readers and are not ability-based groups.

Once Book Club Groups are formed, they meet regularly to read and discuss the books. The teacher rotates through the groups, giving guidance, support, and encouragement. Each day, the groups report to the whole class what has happened or what they have learned in their books so far.

Here is an example using four informational books, *Cats, Wolves, Sharks,* and *Sea Turtles,* all by Gail Gibbons (Holiday House). Because cats are a familiar topic for most children and because there is less text on the pages, *Cats* is an easier book than the other three. *Sea Turtles* is a little harder than *Wolves* and *Sharks.*

The teacher begins Guided Reading today by telling the children that she has found four wonderful, informational animal books. One at a time, she shows the covers of the books. She lets the children tell what they know about each of the four animals and share some of their personal experiences with them. Using only the covers, she gets the children to think about what they know and what they might learn. Then, she tells the children that they have only this week to spend on these books, and the class only has seven copies of each book. Everyone will not be able to read all four books, but they will read one book in their Book Club Groups and hear about the animals in the books the other groups are reading.

Next, the teacher hands each child an index card. She asks the children to write their names and the numbers 1, 2, and 3 on the cards. She explains that they will have 20 minutes to preview the books—five minutes for each book. At the end of the 20 minutes, they will return to their seats and write down their first, second, and third choices.

She places all copies of each book in four separate areas. Then, she divides the class into four random groups and sends a group to each area. She sets a timer for five minutes and tells the children that when the timer sounds, they must move to the next area and the next group of books.

For the next 20 minutes, the children busily try to read and look at as many pages as they can. Each time the timer sounds and they have to move to the next area, the students may complain that they haven't had enough time. The teacher sympathizes but tells them this time is not for studying the books, it is only to decide which book they most want to read.

When the 20 minutes is up, the children return to their seats to make their choices. It isn't easy! Most protest that they want to read all four books! They have trouble deciding which is their first choice and which is their second choice. The teacher tells them not to worry too much about the order of choices because she can't guarantee they will get their first choice—or even their second choice. There are only seven copies of each book, and the groups need to be about the same size.

After school, the teacher looks at all the cards. First, she looks at the cards of the struggling readers. Four of her five struggling readers have listed *Cats* as one of their choices, so she puts them in the *Cats* group, along with two more able readers who have also chosen *Cats*. One struggling reader chose *Sharks* as his first choice, so the teacher puts him in the *Sharks* group.

Next, she looks at the choices of her most able readers. Five of these children have chosen *Sea Turtles,* and she puts them, along with one fairly fluent reader, in the *Sea Turtles* group. She puts the other children in groups according to their choices and evens out the numbers.

She takes four sheets of chart paper and heads each with the name of one of the books and the names of the children in that group. She then divides each chart into three columns and heads them "K," "W," and "L." (See pages 68-69 for a more-detailed explanation of KWL charts.) She chooses one child in each group to be the leader and do the recording, and she places a star by that child's name. She places the charts in the four reading areas, along with the books. She uses a large paper clip to clip together the pages in the last two-thirds of each book so that the students will not read beyond the first ten pages on the first day.

When the children come in the next morning, they immediately find their names on the charts and know which book they will read. Some are disappointed that they didn't get their first choice. The teacher sympathizes, but points out that the books will be available during Self-Selected Reading next week.

At Guided Reading time, the groups go to their areas and the teacher explains how they are going to work for the next three days. She has done many KWL charts with them, so they know that they brainstorm things they **K**now for the first column and things they **W**ant to learn for the second column. She gives a marker to the leader of each group. She tells the children that the leader will be the "teacher" and lead the group just as she does when the class does KWL's together.

The teacher asks the groups to spend ten minutes putting things they know and want to learn in the first two columns. She sets the timer for ten minutes and circulates between the groups, encouraging each group to list as much as they can in the first two columns. When the timer sounds, she tells them to finish writing what they are writing and then begin reading the book.

The teacher explains that they will now have 20 minutes to read the pages in the first third of the book and add things to the **L**earned column on the chart. They will read each two-page spread to themselves silently or using "whisper" voices, and then list things in the **L** column before going to the next two-page spread.

As the groups work, the teacher helps them decide what to write and reminds them how she writes the information when they do KWL's as a class. She begins with the *Cats* group and spends more time here. Even though there are three pretty good readers in this group, the four struggling readers need support and encouragement. The teacher did, of course, make sure that the leader and "teacher" in this group is one of the more able readers and writers.

At the end of 19 minutes, the teacher signals the groups that they only have another minute and that they should finish writing on the chart. One group has not gotten to the last two-page spread. The teacher tells them they can begin there tomorrow, and they will have to move a little faster.

The last ten minutes are spent with each group sharing what they have learned so far with the rest of the class.

For the next two days, the groups review what they have learned so far, add a few more questions to the "Want to learn" column, read the final two-thirds of the book, and add to the "Learned" column. Each day ends with the groups sharing what they have learned.

On the fifth day, the groups reassemble for the last time. Their task today is to read everything they have listed in the **L** column. Then each student writes the three most interesting things he learned and draws a picture to illustrate the new knowledge. The teacher gives the children a paragraph frame to organize their writing:

I learned a lot about _____. I learned that _____. I also learned that_____. The most interesting thing I learned was _____.

The children work busily to write and illustrate their paragraphs using both the books and the KWL charts. Everyone writes good paragraphs since they know so much about their topic, have the books and KWL chart for support, and use the paragraph frame to help structure their writing.

Steve

I learned a lot about <u>cats</u>. I learned that <u>baby cats are called kittens</u>. I also learned that <u>cats are good pets</u>. The most interesting thing I learned was <u>that cats are good hunters</u>.

Jared

I learned a lot about <u>wolves</u>. I learned that <u>some wolves can run up to 40 mph</u>. I also learned that <u>most male wolves weigh over 100 pounds</u>. The most interesting thing I learned was <u>wolves can talk to each other</u>.

Ashley

I learned a lot about <u>sea turtles</u>. I learned that <u>they live in warm waters</u>. I also learned that <u>turtles lived 200 million years ago</u>. The most interesting thing I learned was <u>the leatherback sea turtle is 7 feet long and it weighs 1000 pounds</u>.

Book Club Groups are a favorite way to organize Guided Reading once the children read well enough that the teacher can find multiple books tied together in some way. **It is also crucial that the teacher has modeled the formats the groups will use** (in this example, KWL charts and paragraph frames). Most teachers find that the children participate eagerly in their Book Club Groups and that the books they didn't get to read are the most popular selections during Self-Selected Reading the following week. It is not unusual for children to read all three of the books their group didn't read. Because each group shares information about their book, the students' knowledge of each book is greatly increased, and they are often able to read books at a higher level than they generally can.

WHOLE CLASS

SMALL GROUP

Everyone Read To... (ERT)

Everyone Read To... (ERT) is a way of guiding the whole class (or a small group) through the reading of a selection. Teachers use ERT when they want the students to do the initial reading on their own, but also want to keep them together to provide guidance and support for that initial reading. **Through this method, the teacher tells students either to read to "find out" or "figure out." They read that segment, and then the teacher follows up on whatever purpose was set by asking questions like:**

> • "What did you find out was making the sky so dark?"
>
> • "What new things did you learn?"
>
> • "What seems to be the problem in this story?"
>
> • "Who figured out what kind of class Miss Nelson had?"

When the information the children are reading for is stated directly on the page, we ask them to read **to find out**. When they have to make inferences, we ask the children to read **to figure out**.

Children tell in their own words what they read, and then everyone goes on to the next segment. For older children, Everyone Read To... is usually silent reading. Because children must develop some reading fluency before they can "read it in their minds," this ERT time with young children is often not silent, but rather "whisper" reading. In ERT, everyone reads the text for themselves in whatever way is appropriate to find out specific things they will then share with the class. Here is an ERT example for the book *Three Cheers for Tacky* by Helen Lester (Houghton Mifflin, 1994).

The teacher and the children have read the title, author's and illustrator's names, and have taken a picture walk through the book. They are now going to do the first reading of the book, and the teacher is going to guide them through each two-page spread, using ERT to help them set a purpose.

For the first page, the teacher reminds the children that during their picture walk, they decided that the penguins were the main characters in the story and that one penguin was always doing things differently from the other five. She says, "Everybody read this page **to find out** more about our penguin characters."

The children read the page to themselves, some without any lip movement and others whisper-reading it. As they finish, the children raise their hands, and the teacher calls on children to tell her what they found out about the penguin characters.

Different children add information until all the relevant facts on the page are given. The children have learned that the penguins are named Goodly, Lovely, Angel, Neatly, Perfect, and Tacky. Tacky is the different one; the teacher and the children repeat the names of the five "normal" penguins and then the name of the "odd bird," Tacky. The students enjoy the names and talk about how the author lets you know right away that Tacky is not going to act, look, or dress like the other five penguins in the story.

They turn the page and the teacher reminds the students that during their picture walk, they concluded from the pictures that the penguins were in school. Now she says, "Everybody read **to find out** what these penguins do in their school and what Tacky does that is different."

Again, the children read silently or quietly. Raised hands let the teacher know when the children are ready to discuss what they have read.

They turn the page again and the teacher reminds the children that they read the sign in the picture ("GREAT PENGUIN CHEERING CONTEST") during their picture walk. The students also talk about how the little picture above each penguin probably indicates how the penguins imagine they would look in the cheering contest. The children read **to find out** what the penguins are planning for their part in the cheering contest.

The teacher leads the class through each two-page spread in this manner. For each spread, she reminds the students of what they learned from the pictures, and then sets a purpose for that page that seems to be "the natural thing" you would want to find out after having pondered these pictures:

- "Everyone read to find out what words they are cheering as they do each of these actions."

- "Everyone read to find out how Tacky did the cheer."

- "Everyone read to find out what the other five penguins told Tacky he had to do if he was going to be on their team."

- "Everyone read to figure out why Tacky is dressed in those funny clothes."

- "Everyone read to figure out if Tacky is ever going to be able to do the cheer."

The reading of the story continues in this way, and the children enjoy the story. Thinking about what they see in the pictures helps the students **to figure out** what the words might say, as well as giving them an idea of what to read for. Reading **to find out** is literal comprehension. Reading **to figure out** is inferential.

The teacher concludes the lesson by telling the children that this is a book that "just demands to be acted out," and they will act it out tomorrow. They quickly look through all the pages of the book again and begin to make some plans for tomorrow. The teacher helps them by asking questions, such as:

> • "What characters will we need for this page?"
>
> • "What will they do?"
>
> • "What will they say?"
>
> • "How will they look?"

The children begin to talk about which characters they want to be. The teacher says that there will be different casts for different pages, and that the students will all play many different parts as the entire book is reenacted.

Sticky Note Reading

INDIVIDUAL

PARTNERS

SMALL GROUP

WHOLE CLASS

Sticky Note Reading can be done by children reading alone, with partners, in small groups, or by the whole class. Children use self-adhesive notes to mark what they find interesting, important, or confusing. Sticky notes work particularly well when children have made predictions, or begun a KWL or other graphic organizer before reading. As the children find something in their reading that proves or disproves a prediction, or needs to be added to the KWL or graphic organizer, they write a word or phrase on the sticky note and place it next to where they found the information. During any follow-up activities, the children can refer to their notes and sometimes read aloud the related information.

Sticky notes can also be used for writing a word the reader couldn't pronounce or for which he didn't know the meaning. Again, the sticky note is placed next to the troublesome word so that when the child tells the word, the sentence in which it occurred can be found easily. The teacher and the other children then can help the child figure out the pronunciation or meaning.

Once children know how to use sticky notes to mark information and troublesome words, you may combine the two by giving them two colors of sticky notes. For example, the children might use yellow notes to mark words or phrases that give information and pink notes for confusing words.

Children have much more to add to the after-reading discussions when they have marked information with sticky notes as they encountered it. They monitor their own comprehension better if they have other sticky notes to mark troublesome words. Children also enjoy reading more because adding brightly-colored sticky notes to pages is fun!

BEFORE- AND AFTER-READING VARIATIONS

Picture Walks

Before reading, the teacher and children take a "picture walk" through the book. The teacher helps the children use the pictures to build important concepts by asking questions, such as:

- "Do you know what this is called (pointing to an ax in the picture)?"

- "What does it look like he is doing here?"

- "What holiday does it look like they are celebrating?"

Based on the responses of the children, the teacher confirms their responses and/or suggests words and phrases:

- "We can call it a hatchet. We can also call it an ax. Have you ever heard someone say they chopped wood with an ax?"

- "Yes, it looks like he is fixing a flat tire. He uses the jack to hold up the car."

- "Yes, they are having Thanksgiving dinner."

Once the targeted word has been used by the children or suggested by the teacher, the teacher sometimes leads the children to look at the print on the page and see if they can find a word which would be especially difficult for them to decode on their own:

"Let's say **Thanksgiving** together. Will the word **Thanksgiving** be a short word or a long word? Yes, **Thanksgiving** will probably be a long word. With what two letters do you think **Thanksgiving** might begin? Say **Thanksgiving** again. What three letters do you expect to see at the end of **Thanksgiving**? Now, look at the print and see if you can put your finger on a word that might be **Thanksgiving**."

This picture walk should be brief, but should help students use the pictures to connect to their own experiences and anticipate what they will be reading. Teachers can also help children develop vocabulary by using some new words and connecting these to the pictures. Children can be led to identify some words in the text that might be impossible for most of them to figure out if they encountered them on their own.

Predictions

A time-tested way to help children access prior knowledge, connect reading to experience, and engage them while reading is to have them make predictions before they begin reading:

1. Many teachers read just the first page or two of a story aloud to children, then stop and ask, "What do you think is going to happen?"

2. All responses are accepted and followed by a question to evoke student thinking: "What makes you think that?"

3. The teacher is very non-judgmental and says things like, "That's an interesting idea. I never thought of that. She could do that, couldn't she?"

Sometimes, teachers record predictions on a chart, writing the initials of the child who made each prediction. With older children, two student "recorders" can write down the predictions.

Helping children make predictions before they read is a powerful strategy. Instead of the teacher setting a purpose and telling the children for what information to read, the children learn to set their own purpose. This is what "real" readers do. They begin making predictions from the minute they see the title and cover of a book. As they read the first several pages, they think ahead about what may happen. Sometimes, a prediction is very specific ("If he takes that job working for his father-in-law, the marriage will never make it!"). Other times, a prediction is more general ("Uh, oh! There is going to be trouble here!").

Predictions sometimes prove true, while at other times, the reader is surprised. When helping children make predictions, don't emphasize whether the predictions are right or wrong. Rather, put the emphasis on the prediction making sense. Sometimes, the teacher may even tell the children that their predictions were wonderful, and the author may have written a more interesting story if he had used the plot they predicted!

The importance of predictions is not whether they are right or wrong, but that they are made. Once children have made predictions, their attention is engaged and their comprehension is enhanced. Teachers produce motivated, active, engaged readers when they regularly help children make predictions based on the cover, title, first few pages, and illustrations of a book, and then follow the reading by discussing which predictions really happened and what surprises the author had in store.

KWL's

Perhaps the most effective and popular way of helping children access prior knowledge and make predictions for informational text is the KWL Chart (Ogle, 1986; Carr and Ogle, 1987). **The letters stand for what we Know, what we Want to learn, and what we have Learned.** Here is an example of KWL using *Animal Tracks* by Arthur Dorros (Scholastic, 1991).

The lesson begins with the teacher directing students' attention to the pictures of animals and tracks on the cover of the book. He asks the children what they know about tracks. The children respond that they have seen animal tracks in the snow, on a dry sidewalk, or when the dog comes in the house with dirty feet!

On a large piece of chart paper, the teacher has labeled three columns, "K," "W," and "L." He writes what the children know under the "K" column. They know that birds leave tracks, and so do animals and people. They know that the tracks are made by the animals' feet or paws. They know that animals leave different kinds of tracks depending on their feet. Big animals leave big tracks, and small animals leave small tracks.

Next, the teacher asks the children what they want to learn about animal tracks. One child says he wants to know if all animals leave tracks. Another child wants to know how you can tell which animal has left the tracks. The teacher writes these two questions in the "W" column.

KWL		
<u>K</u>now	<u>W</u>ant to Learn	<u>L</u>earned
Birds make tracks.	Do all animals make	
Animals make tracks.	tracks?	
People can make tracks.	How can you tell which	
Tracks are made by the	animal has left the	
feet or paws of animals.	tracks?	
Different animals leave		
different kinds of tracks.		
Big animals make big		
tracks.		
Small animals make		
small tracks.		

The teacher tells the class that today they will read *Animal Tracks* with partners to see if their two questions are answered in the book, and to see what other new things they can learn to add to the "L" column. If they finish reading before the time is up, they should discuss the answers to the two questions and write down things to add to the "L" column.

The teacher explains that *Animal Tracks* is kind of a "puzzle" book. Each page ends with a question about who made the tracks. The question is answered on the next page. He tells the children to try to answer the question before turning the page. He calls out the names of children who will be partners and reminds them to read in whisper voices. He reminds the partners to help each other figure out words rather than just telling what the word is.

After the children finish their reading, the teacher calls them all back together to complete the last column. The children list new information they have learned, and the teacher records it on the chart.

Whatever the teacher does before reading to set up comprehension must be followed up after reading. Here is the KWL chart one class completed together after reading.

KWL		
Know	Want to Learn	Learned
Birds make tracks. Animals make tracks. People can make tracks. Tracks are made by the feet or paws of animals. Different animals leave different kinds of tracks. Big animals make big tracks. Small animals make small tracks.	Do all animals make tracks? How can you tell which animal has left the tracks?	All animals that walk can make tracks. You can tell what animal made the tracks because the tracks look like the animal's feet. You need water or soft ground to see tracks.

Graphic Organizers

Another popular before-reading strategy for informational text is to start a web, data chart, or other graphic organizer. **To decide which graphic organizer to use, the teacher reads the book and determines what the important information is and how it can best be organized and displayed.**

Many informational texts lend themselves to several different graphic organizers. The following examples are based on the book, *Wonderful Worms* by Linda Glaser (Milbrook Press, 1992).

Web

Looking through this book, the teacher notices important information about earthworms: what they look like, where they live, how they dig, how they move, what they eat, and how they are helpful. She organizes and displays this information on a web drawn on a piece of large paper, an overhead projector transparency, or on the chalkboard. She writes the topic, "Earthworms," in the large center circle. Spokes lead from the center circle to six smaller circles with the words **look**, **live**, **dig**, **move**, **eat**, and **help**. The teacher will add spokes to these smaller circles with the information the children give her after reading the book.

A web is a wonderful way to organize information so that young children can see what they are learning through reading. Graphic organizers, like a web, help children to become active readers when they search for more information about the topics displayed on the web.

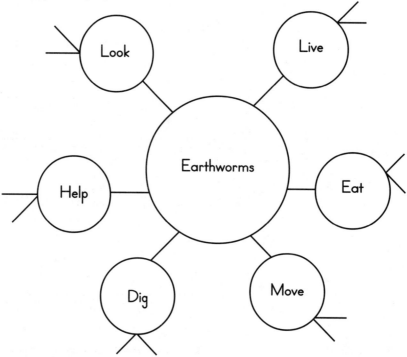

Comparison Charts

Another way to organize the information in *Wonderful Worms* is with a chart that has two columns. The first column is labeled "Worms." The second column is labeled "Us." The headings underneath are "Where They Live," "Body Parts," "How They Dig," and "What They Eat." Children read to find out information about worms, and then add information about themselves from prior knowledge.

	Worms	Us
Where They Live		
Body Parts		
How They Dig		
What They Eat		

Story Maps

Story maps are graphic organizers that help students organize information from stories they read. Story maps help children think about important story elements, including setting, characters, and plot. The story mapping format begins with the name of the book and the author, then the setting (where and when), characters (who), the problem, story events (beginning, middle, and end), and conclusion are all added to the map.

Before reading, the teacher and the students talk about each box on the story map. The teacher tells the students that they will fill in the map together after reading. Children who finish reading before the group comes back together should take notes on things they think belong in the different boxes on the map. There are many different kinds of story maps. One possible format is shown below.

```
                  My Story Map
Name of story/book _____
Author _____

┌──────────────────────────────────────┐
│ Setting:     When          Where      │
│                                        │
└──────────────────────────────────────┘
┌──────────────────────────────────────┐
│ Characters:        Who                 │
│                                        │
└──────────────────────────────────────┘
┌──────────────────────────────────────┐
│ Problem:                               │
│     Beginning                          │
│     Middle                             │
│     End                                │
└──────────────────────────────────────┘
┌──────────────────────────────────────┐
│ Conclusion:                            │
│                                        │
└──────────────────────────────────────┘
```

The Beach Ball

The Beach Ball is not a story map, but can lead to the development of written story maps. The teacher uses a large beach ball with a question written in black permanent marker on each colored stripe of the ball:

- What is the book title and who is the author?
- Who are the main characters?
- What is the setting?
- What happened in the story?
- How did the story end?
- What was your favorite part?

After reading a story, the teacher and children form a large circle. The teacher begins by tossing the ball to one of the students. The first student to catch the ball may answer any question on the ball. That student then tosses the ball to another student. This student may add to the answer given by the first student or answer another question. The ball continues to be thrown to various students until all the questions have been thoroughly answered. Some questions, such as those asking children to tell what happened in the story and share their favorite parts, will have many different answers.

The beach ball is a favorite activity in all the classrooms in which it is used, including those with intermediate-aged children. In classrooms where the teacher regularly uses the beach ball to follow up story reading, children begin to anticipate, as they read, the answers they will give to the questions on the stripes. These children have developed a clear sense of story structure, and their comprehension (and memory!) increases as they organize what they read by thinking about the questions written on the beach ball stripes.

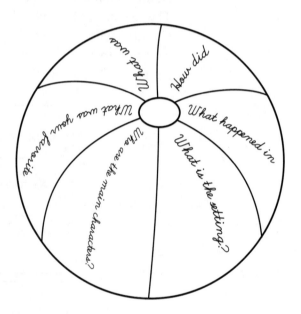

"Doing" the Book

Kids love to "do" things and that includes reading. A popular follow-up to reading is the reenacting of the selection, with various children playing different parts as the rest of the class reads or tells the story.

Here is an example for *Three Cheers for Tacky*. The first reading of this book was described in the ERT section (see pages 62-64). Now, it is time for the second reading. All children will get to act out the penguins' roles since the actors will change every five or six pages.

The teacher has made penguin pictures on which are written the penguin names, Goodly, Lovely, Angel, Neatly, Perfect, and Tacky. She distributes these six name tags to six children and asks these children to come to the front of the class. The rest of the children and the teacher read the sentences together, stopping when actions are indicated for any or all of the penguins.

The class reads, "There once lived a group of penguins in a nice, icy land. One was Goodly." The child with the Goodly name tag steps forward, looking proud. "One was Lovely." The child playing Lovely steps forward, looking very proud.

One at a time the penguins are introduced and step forward. When Tacky steps forward, he looks not proud but "tacky." (The actors may need some direction from the teacher on how to look proud, tacky, etc.)

On the next pages, the teacher and children read about how the penguins go to school. The students act like they are reading books, writing their names, and learning their numbers. Tacky, of course, reads, writes, and does numbers quite differently from the other five penguins.

After five pages, the teacher and the class applaud the actors. Then, these actors take their seats so another group of students can become penguins. The new penguins put on the name tags and act out the next several pages in which the penguins practice cheers for the cheering contest. The teacher chooses a third set of penguins for the next several pages of cheering practice.

For the final pages of the book, all the children are needed as actors. The teacher gives the Goodly, Lovely, Angel, Neatly, Perfect, and Tacky name cards to children who have not yet had them and then gives someone a Judge card. There are three other teams in the competition, so the teacher divides the remaining children into these three teams. With the teacher doing the reading now, one team of penguins does their cheer, and the judge looks bored. The second team does their cheer, and the judge yawns. The third team does their cheer, and the judge snores. Finally, Tacky's team does their cheer. Tacky's odd antics wake up the judge, and his team captures the prize!

Building comprehension strategies is a major goal of Guided Reading. When children "do" the book, they think about all the important story elements— characters, settings, actions, and sequence of events. The benefits of acting out the book as a regular Guided Reading format become obvious when the children come to expect that they will act out the reading selection. If the children know they might act out the story, they think about who they would like to be from the story and what they would do if they were those characters. This kind of thinking greatly increases their comprehension.

"Doing" the book is especially helpful for children who are not fluent in English. Watching and being part of the enactment helps build vocabulary and gives children a nonthreatening way to practice their reading and English skills.

Writing Connected to Reading

There are a variety of ways in which writing can be used to increase comprehension:

- The paragraph frame described as the culminating activity for Book Club Groups (page 61) is one way to increase comprehension.

- Sometimes the writing is shared writing, as when the class made their own book after reading *Moonbear's Books* (page 50).

- Children practice writing when they write down the ideas they want to add to a KWL, story map, or graphic organizer. These completed KWL charts, story maps, and graphic organizers can also be used as frames for story summaries or informational paragraphs.

All children have opinions, and they love to tell you what they think. Writing "prompts," which ask for their opinions, might include the following:

- My favorite part was when...

- My favorite character was ...

- I liked (did not like) this book because...

- The funniest part was when...

- The most interesting things I learned were...

Writing can also be used to help children think beyond the text. After reading *Three Cheers for Tacky* (see pages 62-64), children might do one of the following activities:

- Write a different ending.

- Write about another person or animal they knew who was "different."

- Research and write about real penguins.

MAKING THE GUIDED READING BLOCK MULTILEVEL

Guided Reading is the hardest block to make multilevel. Any reading selection is going to be too hard for some children and too easy for others. There is no need to worry about those children for whom grade-level Guided Reading material is too easy, because the other three blocks get three-quarters of their block time and provide many beyond-grade-level opportunities. In addition, end-of-year testing always indicates that students in Four-Blocks classes who begin first grade with high literacy levels read well above grade-level at the end of the year.

Teachers do, however, need to be concerned about those students for whom grade-level selections are too hard. To make this block meet the needs of children who read below grade level, teachers make a variety of adaptations. **Guided Reading time is not spent on grade-level material all week.** Rather, teachers choose two selections—one at the average reading level of the class and one that is easier—to read each week. The shared reading of a big book is always a good selection for the "easier" reading. In Book Club Groups, teachers should try to have one of the choices be an easier—but still appealing—book.

When using a book or story, the class usually reads each selection several times, reading each time for a different purpose in a different format. Rereading enables children who couldn't read it fluently the first time to achieve fluency by the last reading. Children who need help are not left to read by themselves but are supported in a variety of ways. Most teachers use reading partners, and teach children how to help their partners rather than do all their reading for them. While some children read the selection by themselves and others read with partners, teachers usually meet with small groups of children to help them with reading and comprehension. This variety of formats helps below-level readers achieve some success and learn important reading strategies.

Teachers also provide additional easy-reading time for children whose reading level is well below even the easier selections. Some teachers meet with children individually, or in small groups, while the rest of the children are engaged in centers or other activities. Sometimes, teachers arrange for tutors to work individually with children, or they coordinate with early intervention teachers. One way or another, teachers should make sure that children are getting the support they need, including some coaching each week as they read material at their instructional level.

Kids' Comments about Guided Reading:

"I like Guided Reading because it helps me learn to read."

"I like Guided Reading because I love to find out what happens in the story."

"I like Guided Reading because I get to read with a partner."

"I like Guided Reading because we learn how to help each other."

"I like Guided Reading when we act out the stories."

"I like Guided Reading when we learn about new things."

The pages at the end of this chapter will provide you with a summary and review of information. There is an example of how one week in this block might look. Finally, there is a checklist many teachers use when they begin implementing this framework.

SUMMARY OF THE GUIDED READING BLOCK

The purpose of this block is to build comprehension and fluency with reading, and to introduce students to a variety of literature, including stories, informational text, and poetry.

Total Time: 30–40 minutes

10 min.

Segment One: Before Reading

1. The teacher introduces and supports grade-level and easier text in a number of ways over multiple days:

   - building on student's prior knowledge about the text and topic.
   - beginning graphic organizers, such as webs and story maps.
   - guiding picture discussion and prediction.
   - discussing key vocabulary in context.

2. The teacher focuses the lesson on a comprehension skill or strategy.

15-20 min.

Segment Two: Reading

1. The teacher provides flexible grouping of all students to read the text. Grouping may be paired (partner), individual, small groups reading with the teacher, three-ring circus, or Book Club Groups and can include special teachers or volunteers.

2. The children read the selections. The teacher listens to children reading, coaching those who need help and sometimes taking anecdotal notes.

5-10 min.

Segment Three: After Reading

The teacher directs the whole group in closure activities to match the purpose. These activities may include the following:

- discussion of text/literature.
- acting out the story.
- writing in response to reading.
- completion of a KWL or other graphic organizer.
- discussion of the skill or strategy introduced in Segment One.

GUIDED READING

A TYPICAL WEEK IN THE GUIDED READING BLOCK

Monday

> Grade-Level Selection: "Dinosaurs on the Road" from *Dinosaurs Travel: A Guide for Families on the Go* by Laurie Krasny Brown and Marc Brown (Little, Brown and Company, 1988).

Segment 1: Before Reading

Activating Prior Knowledge: The teacher tells briefly about a cross-country trip she and her family took last summer and how they planned their trip. She shows a couple of pictures taken en route. She asks the students if they have ever taken a trip, and a few students tell about their experiences. The teacher tells them that they are going to read a story about traveling, but that the family in the story is quite different from theirs.

Picture Walk: The teacher takes the students on a picture walk through the story, pointing out key vocabulary words such as **adventure**, **travelers**, **passengers**, and **ferryboats**. The students are delighted to see that the family in the story is a family of dinosaurs that look and act like people.

Comprehension Mini-Lesson: The teacher explains that some stories are about things that did not really happen. Other selections are written about real people, things, and events. The teacher lists two headings on the board, "Fiction" and "Nonfiction," and gives an example of each. Some features of each are listed under the headings.

Teacher-Supported Reading: The teacher invites the students to join in an echo reading of the first two pages of text. The text and pictures are designed like a comic book, and the teacher wants to be sure that the students understand how to track the print.

Segment 2: Reading

The teacher asks the students to read the text with their assigned partners and to decide together whether the selection is fiction or nonfiction. When they have made their decision, they should come up to the board and put a mark under one of the categories to indicate what they think.

Students read the story in assigned pairs—stronger readers with struggling ones where possible. The teacher moves around the room, listening to the partners and coaching as needed. As pairs finish reading, they discuss whether the story is fiction or nonfiction, and then go to the board to indicate their decision.

Segment 3: After Reading

The teacher calls the students together to sit at the front of the room. They review the features of fiction and nonfiction that were listed earlier on the board and decide that, even though they can learn things about traveling from this selection, the selection is fictional. Dinosaurs don't currently exist and, when they did, they didn't travel in the ways these dinosaurs do.

Tuesday

> **Grade Level Selection: "Dinosaurs on the Road" rereading.**

Segment 1: Before Reading

Activating Prior Knowledge: The teacher reviews why and how the class determined on Monday that the story was fiction. She tells the class that even though the story couldn't happen, there are still many things they can learn about travel from the story.

Comprehension Mini-Lesson: The teacher draws a web on the board and puts the word **transportation** in the middle of it as the topic word. She invites students to list the types of transportation they can remember from their reading yesterday, and she adds them to the web.

Segment 2: Reading

The teacher uses a "three-ring circus" format to reread the selection. The most capable readers read the story by themselves. The teacher reads the selection with six children who need her guidance and coaching to read the story. The other children are assigned new partners and read the story together. Everyone is given 15 minutes to read. If students finish before the time is up, they write ideas they would like added to the web graphic organizer.

Segment 3: After Reading

The whole class reconvenes and adds information to the web. The teacher writes the new information in a different color from what was written before reading and emphasizes how much the children have learned through their reading about transportation. (In their science lesson today, they will take the graphic organizer and categorize the modes of transportation by the kinds of energy they need to operate.)

Wednesday

Grade-Level Selection: "Dinosaurs on the Road" rereading.

Segment 1: Before Reading

Activating Prior Knowledge: The teacher reviews with students the graphic organizer (web) they completed on Tuesday, showing them what they learned from the text about transportation. She tells the students that during math today, they will make a graph on the chalkboard, listing all of the modes of transportation that the children discovered in the story. They will also graph the types of transportation experienced by each class member. She asks what type of transportation they predict will be the one used by most of the class.

Comprehension Mini-Lesson: The teacher tells the children that sometimes information is organized for the reader with headings of bold print, and that these headings help the reader find information quickly. She then has the children turn to the story to see how the modes of transportation are used as headings to organize information.

Teacher-Supported Reading: The teacher invites the students to read chorally the first three headings of "Dinosaurs on the Road." For each heading, the teacher asks, "What do you think the author will tell us in this section?"

Segment 2: Reading

The teacher tells the students that they will read with partners again today. Each pair will be reading about one way that people travel. Since they have talked today about how the story is organized with headings, the students should try to quickly locate their assigned sections.

Using a reading chart that tells students who their reading partners are, the teacher says that the partner whose name is listed first should read the section first. (The teacher has intentionally allowed the stronger of the two readers to be the first to read so that support for decoding will be provided for the weaker reader.) The other partner should come up to the front of the room and draw a slip of paper from a box that will tell which type of transportation he and his partner should read about together. The teacher has written all seven modes of transportation on slips of paper. Several pairs will be reading the same section since there are eleven pairs in the class.

Once the partners have their assignments and have settled down together, the teacher gives them further instructions: "Take turns reading your section after you find it. After you have both read the section, I want you to answer this question: What does the story say is important to remember about traveling by that type of transportation?" The teacher writes the question on the board as the partners draw their assigned types of transportation from the box.

The partners take turns reading their sections to each other, with the stronger reader reading first. As the pairs complete their reading, they begin to decide what was important about traveling that way. During this partner reading and discussion, the teacher listens in on each pair, coaching and making anecdotal notes about their reading.

Segment 3: After Reading

Each pair of students tells the class one important thing to remember about traveling by the type of transportation about which they read. The teacher tells the students that during center time today and tomorrow, she would like for the partners to go to the writing center, where there is material for them to write and illustrate what they discovered about their kind of transportation. When each pair has had a chance to design their page, the class will combine the pages into a class guide book on "Things to Remember When Traveling."

Thursday

> **Easier Selection (Below Grade Level):** *The Wheels on the Bus* by **Raffi (Crown, 1990)**

Segment 1: Before Reading

Activating Prior Knowledge: The teacher reviews the graph made in math class on Wednesday, telling the different modes of transportation used by members of the class. She asks questions that encourage children to interpret information on the graph: Which kind of transportation is used most by class members? Which is used least?

Then, she asks which kind of transportation most of them used today to get to school. The class discovers that most students rode to school on a bus. The teacher tells them that some towns and cities have buses, other than school buses, that help people get where they need or want to go. Today, they will read a story about buses.

Comprehension Mini-Lesson: The teacher tells the students that she is going to share with them something that good readers do when they read. She says that it is something they do no, matter how old they are or how difficult the book is that they are reading—they monitor their reading by stopping often to think about what they have read and to be sure that they understand what they have read. She writes the word **monitor** on the board and then adds, "think about what you read." She tells the children that she will show them how to monitor as they read today.

Teacher-Supported Reading: The teacher reads the first couple of pages of the story and stops to model thinking through what she has just read. She invites the students to read a few pages with her, again stopping at intervals to model monitoring comprehension.

Segment 2: Reading

The teacher tells the students they will read with partners today, except for a small group with which she wants to read. Partners should stop every couple of pages to ask each other questions about what they are reading to be sure they are understand the story. The partners read together while the teacher reads with a group of five students who need extra help with monitoring comprehension.

Segment 3: After Reading

The teacher tells the students what a great job they did monitoring their reading today. She reinforces the kinds of questions she heard students asking each other as they monitored what they read. The teacher plays a recording of the song about which the story was written as the kids sing along.

Friday

Easier Selection: *The Wheels on the Bus* **rereading.**

Segment 1: Before Reading

Activating Prior Knowledge: The teacher starts the Guided Reading Block by playing the song the students heard on Thursday, which is based on the book they are reading.

Comprehension Mini-Lesson: The teacher tells the students that there are many ways stories can be told. They have already experienced two ways with today's story: reading and singing. Today, after they read the story again with their partners, they will act out the story. Drama is another way of telling a story.

Segment 2: Reading

The teacher uses a "three-ring circus" format to reread the selection. The most capable readers read the story by themselves. The teacher reads the selection with six children who can read it with her guidance and coaching. The other children are assigned new partners and read the story together. Everyone is given 15 minutes to read. If students finish before the time is up, they pick a part of the story that they think would be fun to act out for the class and decide how to perform it.

Segment 3: After Reading

The teacher calls the class together and lets various children act out the story as she reads it aloud.

TEACHER'S CHECKLIST FOR GUIDED READING

In preparing and presenting my lesson in this block, I have...

_____ 1. Presented a comprehension skill or strategy before reading and followed it up after reading.

_____ 2. Introduced new material by previewing pictures and making predictions.

_____ 3. Provided grade level and easier material for this block.

_____ 4. Used basals, multiple copies of trade books, big books, and content area materials.

_____ 5. Established prior knowledge by helping students to make connections between the content and what is familiar to them.

_____ 6. Varied the types of materials/texts presented on multiple days during this block.

_____ 7. Established and stated a clear purpose for students' reading and followed this up after reading.

_____ 8. Provided consistent models of the types of higher-level questions that students should ask of themselves, partners, and literacy circles during and after reading.

_____ 9. Arranged grouping during Segment Two (reading) that is flexible and purposeful. Readers who need greater levels of support are paired with stronger readers or work in a small group. No grouping remains stagnant or easily identifiable, especially with struggling readers.

Another way children learn to read is by writing. For some children, their own writing provides the first successful reading experience. Many children love the combination of writing and illustrating that leads to a published work. Children's writing samples, prior to the publication stage, serve as a rich portrait of how well young minds are applying important language skills and strategies, as well as what they know about words.

The Writing Block includes a mini-lesson that provides children with a model of what writers do. During the block, children engage in various writing activities from starting a new piece, finishing a piece, revising, editing, or illustrating. Another component includes conferences that lead to a final published piece. In the Author's Chair, children share their writing and respond to each other's writing at various stages in its development.

THE WRITING BLOCK

Goals:

- **See writing as a way to tell about things.**
- **Write fluently.**
- **Learn to read through writing.**
- **Apply grammar and mechanics in their own writing.**
- **Learn particular forms of writing.**
- **Maintain the self-confidence and motivation of struggling writers.**

One way children learn to read is by writing. For struggling children, their own writing is sometimes the first thing they can read. The daily Writing Block is carried out in "Writers' Workshop" fashion (Graves, 1995; Routman, 1995; Calkins, 1994). **Here are the components of the Writing Block.**

Mini-Lesson—Teacher Writing

The Writing Block begins with a ten-minute mini-lesson. The teacher works with the overhead projector or with a large piece of chart paper. She writes and models all the things writers do—although not all on any one day! The teacher thinks aloud, deciding what to write, and then writes. While writing, the teacher models looking at the Word Wall for a troublesome word which is there, as well as inventing the spelling of a few big words.

Children Writing and Teacher Conferencing

Next, the children work on their own writing. Since children vary in their writing development and the time they need for different tasks, they are at different stages of the writing process—starting a new piece, finishing a piece, revising, editing, or illustrating. While the children write, the teacher conferences with individuals, helping them get pieces ready to publish. In most classrooms, teachers let children publish a piece when they have completed three to five good first drafts. The child chooses one to publish and then conferences with the teacher. At this point, spelling is corrected and mechanics are fixed, so that everyone can easily read the published piece.

Sharing

This block ends with the "Author's Chair," in which several students each day share first drafts or a published piece. It is a time when children can listen to what their peers are writing. What children read in the Author's Chair gives the other children in the class new ideas for their writing.

VARIATIONS WITHIN THE WRITING BLOCK

Depending on the time of year and the grade level, you will see many variations in the Writing Block. Here are a few examples:

"Driting"

Early in first grade, the Writing Block begins with "driting." Preschool children like to pretend they can write. They do this by **combining drawing along with some circle/line letter-like forms, some letters, a few words (sometimes copied from a book, sign, or calendar), and often a few numbers put in where they "look good." The children then proceed to "read" what they have written**, usually to the delight of the parents.

Instruction must begin at the same level where the children are, and many first graders may not have done this driting—drawing and writing—at home, so the first-grade Writing Block they begin with driting.

Procedure

For the mini-lesson, the teacher places a large sheet of drawing paper on the board and then, using crayons, draws a picture and writes a few words to go with it. She says:

> "Each day at this time, I am going to draw and write something I want to tell you. Today, I am drawing a cat because we have a big, gray cat at my house named Tommy. Tommy loves everyone. Tommy climbs on people's laps whether they like cats or not."

As the teacher is saying this, she is drawing a big gray cat and writing the words **cat** and **Tommy**. She may also write, "I love my cat." **In the writing mini-lesson, the teacher tries to model a type of writing which most children can achieve. In most first grades, some children can draw, some can drite, and some are ready to write.**

Next, the teacher gives everyone a piece of drawing paper (without any lines) and directs them:

> "Use your crayons to draw something you want to share with the rest of the class. You can write some words, too, the way I wrote **cat** and **Tommy**, but you don't have to. Draw and write in whatever way you would like, so that you can tell us what you want to share. Your writing doesn't have to be about a cat or a pet. It can be about a person, or something you like to do, or anything that you want to tell us. I am going to give you ten minutes to draw and write. Then, we'll all make a circle and tell about our driting."

As the children draw and write, the teacher encourages them, responding enthusiastically to whatever they are creating, saying things like:

- "Oh, I see someone else has a cat."

- "Dogs are good to write about, too!"

- "I can tell someone in here is a big soccer fan!"

- "Can you tell me about what you are drawing?" (When you haven't the foggiest idea what is being created!)

After ten minutes of driting, the teacher and the children spend 10-15 minutes letting volunteers show their work and talk about it.

How Long to Use "Driting"

Teachers often ask, "How long do you use the driting format?" In some classrooms, where most children have been writing in kindergarten or at home, the Writing Block resembles the description above for only a day or two. In other first grades in which the children have had few experiences with print, driting is the Writing Block variation for a week or two.

To answer the question of when to move on, the teacher has to look at what the children are producing. Are they attempting to write some words to go with their pictures? Each day, when the teacher is doing the driting mini-lesson, she both draws and writes. Usually, early in the year, some children just draw. Other children will find words in their classroom that they can copy (i.e., names, color words) or simply copy the letters in the alphabet that they see above the chalkboard, since they know these letters make words.

Remember, there are three other blocks being used. Words are being added to the Word Wall. Children are learning about letters and sounds as they do different activities from the Working with Words Block, such as *Making Words*, *Rounding Up the Rhymes*, and *Guess the Covered Word*. Children are having daily Guided Reading, and they are reading in whatever way they can during Self-Selected Reading. As time passes, more and more children add words and sentences to their drawings and begin to "really" write. Teachers have also noted that when they start to write a sentence or two, many of the children follow their example.

The Half-and-Half Format

When most of the children are using both words and drawing in their driting, it is time to move on. In most classrooms, that move is signaled by a new kind of paper, which has drawing space on the upper half and a few writing lines on the bottom half. (This paper is called "story paper," and sometimes described as "half-ruled.") Thus, this can be called the half-and-half format.

If children in the second or third grade are reluctant to write, or have not had much experience with the "Author's Chair" format and daily writing, then the half-and-half format is the place to start during the first few weeks of school.

Procedure

When the teacher decides it is time to move to the half-and-half format, she begins her mini-lesson by putting a piece of half-and-half paper on the board (or a half-and-half-transparency on the overhead). She says something like:

"You're learning to read and write so many words that, starting today, we're going to use this writing and drawing paper for our writing. You'll still write and draw what you want to tell us, but you can do your writing here (points to the lines) with your pencil, and then you can draw your picture here (points to the blank part of the paper) with your crayons. If you want to draw your picture first, that is fine also." (Some children find more to say when they look at the picture they have drawn.)

The teacher then models this procedure. She writes a simple sentence or two (not more!) the first time, modeling how to look at the Word Wall for words she knows are there and stretching out other words. Then, she draws a picture that goes with the writing.

Next, the children do their writing. Some children draw first and just write their names. Others write a few words and draw. Some write a few sentences. One child might write a whole page. The teacher goes around and encourages students. If asked to spell a word, she does not spell it, but rather helps the child stretch the word out and write at least some letters.

After 10-15 minutes, the teacher gathers the children in a circle to share their creations, just as they did when driting. The teacher responds positively to what they tell, including to those few children who only have a picture! In a few weeks, with the help of the Word Wall, other words around the room, and a few coaching sessions with the teacher to help them stretch out words, even the struggling children will generally write a sentence or two to go with their pictures.

Writing, Revising/Editing, and Publishing

The next move is from the half-and-half format to the format in which children are writing on their own without teacher encouragement. The teacher can now spend the 15-20 minutes when the children are writing to help them revise, edit, and publish pieces. This is also the time when she begins to use the Author's Chair procedure in which the Monday children share on Monday one piece they have written since the previous Monday, the Tuesday children share on Tuesday, and so on.

Once most of the children are writing, many teachers let the students choose the kind of paper they would like to use. Some teachers help their students to think about which paper will help them tell their story best: plain, half-and-half, formal handwriting paper ruled with the appropriate grade level lines, or notebook paper. (This could be another mini-lesson!) Some classes use lined notebooks for all their writing. These teachers have the children—those who can write on the lines—use every other line so that there is plenty of room left to edit. Of course, many young children cannot write on the lines, but they still enjoy writing in their notebooks.

Once a class is writing, revising/editing, and publishing, there are some additional variations:

- **In most classrooms, teachers let children publish a piece when they have completed three to five good first drafts.** (Of course, "good" is a relative term which varies from child to child!) When the child has the required number of first drafts, he chooses one to publish. If he is in second or third grade, he then chooses a friend to help with the revising and editing, or he does some self-editing. Once this is done, the child signs up for a conference with the teacher, who helps the writer get the piece into publishable form. At this point, all spelling is fixed and the piece is "tidied up" mechanically, because a published piece should be something that everyone else can read easily, and of which the child will be proud.

- While many teachers find the above procedure quite workable, **other teachers prefer to work with a third of their class each week**. These teachers divide the class into thirds, including one of their most able and least able writers in each third. In week one, children in the first third edit and publish a piece while the other two-thirds of the class work on as many first drafts as they can in a week. In week two, when the first third have published a piece, they go back to first-draft writing while the teacher works with the second third. In week three, the final third (who have been producing first drafts for two weeks and may have a lot from which to choose) get to publish a piece. Week four finds the first third back into their writing/ conferencing/publishing cycle.

- **There are variations in the publication form, too**, including individual books; pieces copied, illustrated, and displayed on a class author board; class books; pieces typed and illustrated using a computer publishing program; and even some class-created web pages.

Regardless of how the writing, revising/editing, and publishing process is structured, it is important that children spend more of their writing time doing the difficult (but important!) work of first-draft writing. It is during this time that children do a lot of the mental work—applying everything they are learning during the other three blocks—that moves them along in reading and writing:

- As children use the Word Wall and other room resources to spell words and stretch out the spelling of longer words, **they are applying their word and phonics strategies.**

- **Children also apply their comprehension strategies** as they learn to keep their writing on topic, to put things in the right sequence, and to decide if what they write is going to be "real" or "make believe."

- In the beginning most children do not write real stories. Their writing is more descriptive and personal. Once they learn more about stories from their reading, they like to try to write them. As they write stories, **students learn that each story must have a beginning, a middle, and an end. The children also begin to think about story elements, such as characters and setting**.

- **The children also write informational pieces, and they use what they are reading both to get information <u>and</u> to use as models for how to write information.**

A Variety of Mini-Lessons

Mini-lessons begin in a "huddle" in the front of the classroom. The children are close and can see the teacher write as she "thinks aloud" and talks about what she is doing and why. Some teachers let the students sit in their seats to watch and listen. (If you are not getting quiet listeners, then pull them closer. It helps!) **Some mini-lessons are "musts" for all primary classrooms:**

- Choosing a Topic

- What to Do if You Can't Spell a Word

- Punctuation and Grammar

- Adding On to a Piece

- Revising

- Editing

Margaret Defee, the pilot teacher for the Four Blocks, taught us a lot of what we now know about "Author's Chair." She kept a list of the mini-lessons she taught. Please see page 94 for a list of Margaret Defee's mini-lessons.

Mrs. Defee also kept a list of the books her students published during the first year. There were over 200 titles on that list, including these:

I Built a Snowman	**School**	**St. Louis**
My Friends	**When I Moved**	**Space**
The Lost Shoe	**My Joke Book**	**Trick-or-Treating**
The Witch's Brew	**Easter**	**Grandma and Me**
German Shepherds	**Mike Tyson**	**Paul Bunyan**
Winter	**My Race Car**	**Richard Petty**
Swords		**Lightning**

Mini-lessons vary according to grade level and the observed needs of children. Several mini-lessons follow that are essential at the beginning of the year, regardless of grade level and how well students write.

Great Ideas for Mini-Lessons*:

1. Actual class procedures used during the writing period
2. Rules for the writing period made by teacher and/or students
3. Teacher models writing using "think-alouds"
4. Working together with the class on shared writing
5. "Words Authors Use" (Have a word a day. Examples: publish, illustrate, edit, topic, dedicate, etc.)
6. Grammar and Usage

   nouns – words that mean a person, place, or thing

   verbs – words that show action

   adjectives – words that describe
7. Capital letters
8. Punctuation marks
9. How to "Set a Scene" (setting)
10. Fiction
11. Nonfiction
12. Mysteries
13. Stories that teach
14. "Feelings" in writing
15. Read a book, any book! Books are great writing models
16. How to add to or change a story
17. Staying on the topic
18. Rhyming words
19. Synonyms
20. Homonyms
21. Antonyms
22. Poetry (This could turn into a week of mini-lessons.)
23. Letter writing
24. Interviews
25. Riddles
24. Jokes
25. Newspapers
26. How to make a List
27. Student pieces (Always use a piece that a student has down correctly!)

*A successful mini-lesson is short, teacher-directed, and discusses only one topic.

Choosing a Topic

Procedure

The teacher begins this mini-lesson by telling the students, "When you write, you should usually choose topics you know a lot about."

Then, the teacher models how she chooses a topic to write about each day:

> "Today, I could write about my favorite basketball team, Wake Forest University. They are playing the University of North Carolina tonight. When these two teams play each other, it is always a good basketball game...I could write about my daughter's new car. She is so excited about her first new car!...I could also write about my cat, Tommy. He's such a rascal. I told you before that I had a cat named Tommy, but I didn't tell you very much about him. I think I will write about my cat Tommy."

The teacher then begins writing on an overhead transparency or on a large piece of chart paper so that all the children can see. She talks as she writes:

> "I can put the title, My Cat, here at the top because I know that I will write all about my cat. I begin the first sentence with a capital letter: 'My cat's name is Tommy.' I begin **Tommy** with a capital letter also because names begin with capitals.

> "He is fat and furry, so I am going to write that for my second sentence. Once again I am going to begin with a capital letter for the first word in the sentence. I can spell **fat** but I am not sure of **furry**. Let me stretch out the word **furry** and listen for the letters that make those sounds: '**f-ur-re**.' When I am writing a new word and I am not sure that I spelled it correctly, I write it the best I can, then I circle it. That means I will check that word if I decide to publish this story later."

The teacher continues to talk about her cat and writes what she is saying:

> "He likes everyone. He thinks everyone likes him. Tommy is a rascal." (Stretching it out, she spells the last word **raskl**.)

After having written her five sentences, the teacher asks the students to tell her things they know a lot about. Hands go up and the list begins. The children tell her about their pets, parents, friends, and other topics in which they are interested. She concludes by saying, "Those all sound like good story topics to me! So let's tiptoe back to our seats and begin to write about them."

Topic Chart

Some teachers keep a chart in the room on which, throughout the day, they write topics about which they and the children might like to write. For example, when a child comes in with new glasses, the teacher comments on them and adds "glasses" to the chart.

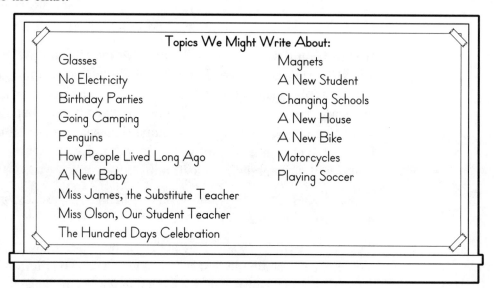

Topics We Might Write About:

Glasses	Magnets
No Electricity	A New Student
Birthday Parties	Changing Schools
Going Camping	A New House
Penguins	A New Bike
How People Lived Long Ago	Motorcycles
A New Baby	Playing Soccer
Miss James, the Substitute Teacher	
Miss Olson, Our Student Teacher	
The Hundred Days Celebration	

Examples

Writing, by its nature, is a multilevel activity, offering all children an opportunity to do what they can! Here are several children's responses, early in first grade, to the Choosing a Topic mini-lesson:

My cat is fat and furry.
He is funny and playful.
He is curios. He get's in trouble.
(Wade)

MY CAT
I have a cat.
Hre name is smoke.
She's my on cat.
I love hre a lote.
(Meredith)

My Mommy
My Mommy is nice. She
is pritty.
I love her a lot. We
play togathr a lot.
My Mommy wrks a lot.
She works at the
frmace.
(Stephanie)

I have a big dog.
My dog slep in my bed with my and
mom.
Me and my dog we go otsid wrin
my mom seys we can go otsid.
(Brittany)

What to Do When You Can't Spell a Word

When elementary school students write, they cannot spell all the words they want to use unless they limit what they say to words they can spell. Children can and will choose "easy" words if the teacher (or a parent) talks too much about spelling it "right." When children limit their word choices, they no longer write about an **enormous** dinosaur, but a **big** one. Food is not **delicious**, it is **good**. Friends are not **fantastic** or **wonderful** to play with, they are **nice**. **Children, whether eager or reluctant writers, need to feel free to express themselves and use the words they want to tell their stories.**

The Word Wall and other visible words in the room will help with lots of words, but there are many words young children have in their speaking vocabularies that are not in their reading or writing vocabularies. For these words, ask children to do what authors (and adults) do: say the word slowly and listen for the sounds they hear, then write the letters those sounds represent. Sometimes adults are right, and sometimes they are wrong. . . just like children! So, they circle the word and check on it later.

It is a good idea to have a mini-lesson on "what to do when you can't spell a word" early in the school year. After that, model what you do about spelling for several words—but not all the words—in each mini-lesson.

For this example mini-lesson, the teacher takes a big piece of chart paper or an overhead transparency and begins to talk and write:

"Today, I am going to write about the snow we had yesterday. I'm beginning with a capital letter because sentences begin that way. Yesterday was January 28. I can find the words **January** and **yesterday** on our calendar board. **January** is at the top; it is the name of this month. I know that under the calendar it says, 'Today is_____. Yesterday was _____. Tomorrow will be _____.' So I can look there and find the word **yesterday**.

"Once again, for the second sentence, I start with a capital letter and write, 'We had (**had** is easy because I can look on the Word Wall for it) six (the word **six** is one of the number words in the front of our classroom) **inches** (I look around the room for the word inches, and I don't see it. If it's not on the Word Wall, and I cannot find it anywhere in the room, I'll stretch it out and sound-spell the word: **i-n. . . c-h. . . e-s**.) of snow (I can find **snow** on the theme board where all the winter words are listed under winter pictures)."

The teacher follows the same thinking process when she writes her next three sentences:

"I made snowballs. I made a snowman. I had fun in the snow."

It is important to show children what adults and good writers do when they need a word they can't spell. **Authors don't stop their writing and look up a word. They keep writing, spell the word the best they can, and check it later.** Young children need to learn to have a spelling consciousness—that means spelling words as best as they can in the first draft and correcting them in the final draft. **Looking up words in the dictionary belongs in the editing stage, not the first draft.**

Adding On to a Piece

How can teachers get children to continue a story the next day? Continue a story in your mini-lesson, modeling the thought processes involved. For example, the teacher who wrote about the cat named Tommy (see page 95) continues her story the second day. She tells the children that she did not write everything she knew about her cat, and there are a lot more things she could tell. She could tell where he likes to sleep and what he likes to eat. She could tell some stories about times when Tommy thought he was a person and acted just like one.

Then, she takes out her piece from the day before, rereads what she has already written, and adds on to the story by starting a second paragraph:

My cat thinks he is a person. He likes to sleep on the bed. He puts his head on the pillow, just like I do! He likes to eat spaghetti. Sometimes he eats popcorn if it falls on the floor.

The teacher can continue the piece for a third day if she thinks her class is ready for more (maybe about a time Tommy surprised everyone and made them laugh). When writing longer pieces, the teacher can edit the paragraphs daily during the minilesson or spend the fourth day revising and editing all three. **There is no right or wrong time frame for this mini-lesson. Look at your students' writing to see what they need.**

First Day

My Cat

My cat's name is Tommy. He is fat and (furre). He likes everyone. He thinks everyone likes him. Tommy is a (raskl)

My cat thinks he is a person. He likes to sleep on the bed. He puts his head on the pillow, just like I do! He likes to eat spaghetti. Sometimes, he eats popcorn if it falls on the floor.

Second Day

MINI LESSON

Editing Checklist: Capitalization and Punctuation

Many states or school systems have a list of required "language skills" which usually include punctuation, capitalization, and grammar. For years, these language skills were taught with worksheets and workbooks, but there was little transfer to students' writing. **Now we know that if language skills are to transfer to writing, they must be taught during writing.** Some mini-lessons should focus on the language skills of punctuation, capitalization, and grammar.

For punctuation, capitalization, and grammar, develop and gradually add to an editing checklist like the one at right.

Note that items are added gradually. The first thing this teacher put on the checklist was, "Name and date." This was the only thing on the checklist. Each day as the teacher finished whatever writing she was doing for her mini-lesson, she pointed to the checklist and asked the children to help her check to see if she had included her name and the date. Some days, she had put both. Some days, she had put her name but not the date, or the date but not her name. On other days, she had put neither. The children soon got in the habit of checking her writing for this and loved pointing out to her when she had "forgotten!"

1. Name and date
2. Sentences make sense
3. Ending .?!
4. Beginning capitals
5. Capitals for names
6. Possible misspellings circled
7. Title in center
8. Stays on topic

Once the teacher began the checklist, she also began asking children to check their papers each day before putting them away. In a week's time, almost all the children were automatically putting their names and the date on their papers every day. Those who forgot one or the other quickly added it when the writing time was up and the teacher prompted them to check for it.

When almost all the children have learned automatically to do one important "mechanical" thing, it is time to add a second item. The teacher in the example added "Sentences make sense," and from that day on, the children helped her check her writing for two things: Had she remembered to put her name and date, and did all the sentences make sense? During this time, she would usually write one sentence which did not make sense, either by leaving out a word, putting in a wrong word, or failing to finish the sentence. After checking for the name and date, the teacher and the children would read each sentence together and decide if it made sense and, if not, how to fix it.

Once there were two things on the list, the teacher asked the children to read their own writing each day to see that they had included their names and dates, and that all their sentences made sense. Sometimes it takes about a month for the children to get in the habit of checking for these two things in their own writing. When the teacher notices that most children do this, it is time to add another item to the checklist. The children don't always find the sentences that don't make sense ("It made sense to me!"), but they know that writers reread their pieces to check for this.

Take signals from the children for adding to the checklist. Don't expect them to become perfect at executing each item on the list, but watch for them to know what they should be checking. **As the checklist gets longer, and what the children write each day gets longer, they can't check for everything every day. Rather, they use the editing checklist to check their own first-draft writing before conferencing with the teacher.**

Parts of Speech

In addition to using the editing checklist, which is a part of almost every mini-lesson, **some mini-lessons should focus on the parts of speech—nouns, verbs, and adjectives and their functions—which is part of most primary language curriculums**. Most teachers begin to do some grammar mini-lessons during second grade. Again, take cues from the children. When children are writing fluently, it is time to help them begin to look for better ways to say things.

One teacher who did this quite well was a second-grade teacher who wrote a story one day and then read it to her class.

- The class then talked about nouns being words for people, places, and things. They looked for nouns in each sentence. Then the teacher asked, "Could I have used a better word than **dog**? Could I have said it was a **dalmatian** or a **dachshund**? When I wrote, 'the dog ran down the street,' could I have used a better noun than **street**? Was it a highway, a busy neighborhood street, or a country road?"

- After looking for the nouns and replacing them with more specific, more descriptive words and phrases, the teacher talked about verbs, or action words. She then asked, "When I wrote, 'the dog ran down the street,' should I have said, 'he scampered,' or, 'he dashed'?"

- **The teacher helped the children see that using more specific nouns and verbs helps readers see your story better.** She reminded them, "When you write today, or if you are revising, remember to look at the nouns and verbs and see if you can make your story even better!"

Many of her students were soon looking at their own pieces and adding "better" nouns and verbs.

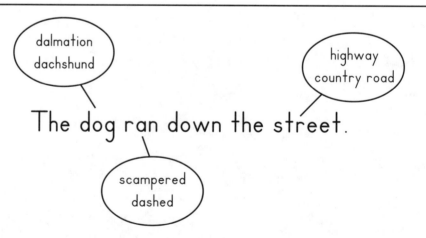

One student in particular put into practice many of the skills from these mini-lessons. He first wrote an informational piece about bichon puppies. Then he wrote a story about a bichon puppy, titled, "A Long Ride Home." It is always rewarding when teachers can see firsthand that the students are becoming better at writing!

Bichons by Brandon

A Bichon is a kind of dog. You can't be allergic to them, they do not shed and they are good with children. A Bichon puppy is about three inches long. You need to put a collar on them when they are 6 weeks old.

When they are puppies you will need to get them a chew toy because they will want to chew. A full-grown Bichon is about 1 foot tall and 24 inches long. They are really cute. When they are about 2 years old they will probably act like a kid. When they are puppies they will want to use paper. When they are older they will go outside to the bathroom.

A Long Ride Home by Brandon

One cold December day a Bichon mom named Bunny was having babies. They were born on December 10th. The runt of the group was named Frisco. He was the last one out of the mom. He was the first to get out of the box and the first one to go use the paper.

One January day a nice family of five came to bring him home. The boy's name was Weavil. The Weavils went in the house, got the puppy, went out, and got in the car. They soon left.

First the family stopped by a restaurant and got some food. They got home in two hours. Frisco was very excited, so he ran around. He was very happy to be at his new home. THE END

MINI LESSON

Revising and Editing

Many teachers write and edit during their mini-lessons every day, especially in first grade, where the pieces they model are as short as the pieces the children write. As the students' pieces get longer and longer, so do the teachers'. That makes writing and editing all in ten minutes more difficult. **Many second- and third-grade teachers spend several days on a piece: writing, adding on, and making it better with revisions and editing.**

Other teachers show the class several "good" pieces written by children in the class and then edit one of the pieces to show just how it is done. There is one rule for this: **It should not be an example of the best or the worst.** In one second-grade class, a boy wrote a piece about dinosaurs. He was such a good writer that it needed almost no revision or editing. A piece such as this is not a good piece to choose to model revising and editing, but it is a delight to the teacher and children.

Velociraptor

2 Velociraptor were hunting. They had seen a triceratops. A raptor pounced and became locked in combat too fierce for the other to enter. After a long battle neither of the two animals had won, both had killed the other in battle leaving the other raptor on his own. After scavenging some meat, he left in search of a new herd. A few days later the raptor had spotted a protoceratops nest. The eggs make an easy meal if it wasn't for one problem, an oviraptor. The slightly smaller predator was also eating the eggs, so the raptor would have to fight for a meal. The raptor moved toward the nest, then, slashing out with it's sickle-claws the velociraptor pounced scaring away the enemy and an easy fast-food stand. As the raptor feasted it heard a roar. Suddenly a Turbasaurus burst into view. The raptor saw another herd chasing Turbasaurus. The raptor decided to join the hunt. With his help, the herd brought down prey. He had found a pack.

Don't choose a piece that is hard to read or understand. **Choose something that is "good" and needs some work in order to be published.** This way, the students can enjoy reading the piece and learn how to edit (peer edit or self-edit) at the same time. Below is a story that a teacher used early in second grade to demonstrate this.

1. First, the teacher made a photocopy of the piece. Then, she made a transparency from the copy.

2. Using the transparency on the overhead projector, she let the children read the original and tell the author what they liked about it.

3. Next, she asked for any suggestions the children might have for ways to make it better. The children made suggestions for more specific words and a few sentences to add. The writer decided which suggestions to use in revising.

4. Finally, the children made editing suggestions, such as fixing spelling, re-writing run-on sentences, and correcting some punctuation.

Rough Draft

My Cat Filex by Sarah

My cat's name is Filex. He same times palys arouad the house. He is funny. He sads on his bach feet when I hold chees in the air. And one time he juped up on the calner to get some cik-noodl soop. He likes me and my family. He like chees too. He is lasy some-times.

Final Draft

My Cat Felix
by Sarah

My cat's name is Felix. He sometimes plays around the house. He is funny. He sits on his back feet when I hold cheese in the air. One time Felix jumped on the counter to get some chicken noodle soup. He likes my family. Felix likes cheese too. Sometimes, he is lazy. But I still like my cat Felix!

FOCUSED WRITING

Most of the writing done during the Writing Block follows the format just described. Teachers model a variety of topics and forms (genres) during the mini-lessons, but children choose their own topics and decide on the forms they want to use.

Sometimes, however, the teacher wants all the children to write about a specific topic or to learn to write a specific form. Alert children ahead of time that next week during writing time they will all be working on some writing as a class, but that when the week is over they will be able to get back to their own topics. Following are examples of two focused writing weeks at the end of the first grade or during second or third grade.

Letters—Focused Writing

The teacher of this class has a good friend who is a teacher in a faraway state. The two teachers decide that their students would enjoy being pen pals and exchanging letters. The class is excited about the idea—this is their first letter-writing experience. The teacher wants them to learn the correct form for a letter, while at the same time making sure the emphasis is kept on the message.

1 **Brainstorming**
The lesson begins with the teacher asking the children what kinds of things they would like to know about their pen pals. He records these questions on a large sheet of paper:

Questions about pen pals:
- How old is he/she?
- What is school like there?
- Do they have a gym?
- Do they have a lot of homework?
- Do they have a basketball team?
- Does he/she play basketball?
- Does he/she play baseball? football? soccer? other sports?
- What is the weather like?
- What do they do with their friends?
- What does he/she like to eat?
- Do they have a computer?
- Do they play video games?

It is clear that the children have many things they would like to know about their new pen pals. The teacher helps them organize their questions by beginning a web like the one at right.

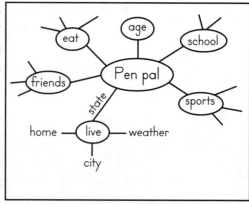

The children help decide where the questions they have already listed should go. Then, they come up with more questions, which are also written in the correct places on the web.

On the following day, the teacher and the children review the web. The teacher points out that, if these are some of the things they would like to know about their pen pals, they are probably also some of the things their pen pals are wondering about them. He explains that they can't possibly include all of this information in the first letter, but that they will be writing back and forth all year. As the year goes on, they will share and learn these kinds of things and many others.

2 **First Draft**
The teacher goes to the overhead and leads the children through the process of writing the first letter. He explains that since this letter will be read by their pen pals, and probably by many other people, each letter must be correct and readable. Today's task is to get a good first draft started which will be edited and recopied or typed later.

The teacher explains and models for the children how and where they put the inside address, date, and greeting. The children watch as he does each step at the overhead. Then, they do the same steps on their papers.

Once these formalities are over, the teacher asks children to look at the web and decide what to write about in the first paragraph. The class decides that they should write about their personal facts. The teacher agrees and has them watch as he writes a paragraph and gives some personal facts about himself.

After writing this first paragraph, the teacher reads it aloud, changing one word and adding another word to model how a writer reads and changes as he writes. He points out the paragraph indentation and has the class notice that his paragraph has four sentences. Then, he instructs the children to write their first paragraphs, telling some personal facts about themselves. He reminds them that first drafts are always on every other line so that there is space to add or change things later.

The children begin to write their paragraphs. As they write, they glance at the web on the board and at the teacher's letter on the overhead. It is clear that, even though these children are not very sophisticated writers, the demonstration they have observed, along with the displayed web and letter, provides the support they need to do a first draft.

When most students have finished their paragraphs, the teacher reminds them that good writers stop occasionally and read what they have written before moving on. He waits another minute while each child reads what has been written. He is encouraged when he sees them making a few changes based on their own rereading.

The process of the teacher writing a paragraph, reading it aloud, making a few changes, and then giving the children time to write their own paragraphs continues that day and the next. The teacher and the children construct paragraphs with information from the categories on the web. After each paragraph, the children are reminded to reread and to make any needed changes or additions. The teacher notices that, when they get to the fifth paragraph, many children are automatically rereading and changing without being reminded to do so.

Finally, the teacher suggests possible closings and shows the children where to put the closing. As they watch, he writes a closing on his letter, then they write theirs. This completes the first draft of the letters.

❸ Revising

On the fourth day, the teacher helps children polish their letters. He puts children into sharing groups of four and has each child read her letter to the others. Just as for the Author's Chair, this sharing is focused on the message only. Listeners tell the author something they liked, and the author asks them if anything was not clear, or if they have suggestions for making it better.

When everyone in the group has had a chance to share, students make whatever revisions they choose. Children can be seen crossing things out and inserting additional information. As they do this, it becomes apparent why it is critical to write the first draft on every other line.

4 **Editing**

Now that the letters are revised and the children are satisfied with their message, it is time to do a final edit. The children are accustomed to choosing a friend to help them edit a draft that they are going to publish, so they tailor this process to letters.

The children refer to the editing checklist displayed in the classroom and decide that the things for which they usually edit are still valid, but that they need to change number 1 to correspond with letter editing. Number 1 had been "Name and date." They decide that for letters, number 1 should be "Address, date, greeting, and closing." The children then pair up with friends and read for each thing on the checklist together. When they have finished helping each other edit, they share their drafts with the teacher during a final editing conference.

5 **Final Copy**

On the following day, students choose some "stationery" from a collection of paper and copy the letters in their most legible handwriting. Finally, the teacher demonstrates how to put the recipient's address and the return address on an envelope. (Even though he intends to mail them all to the pen pals' school in one big envelope, he wants the children to learn how to address envelopes. He also knows that individually sealed envelopes will help the pen pals feel that they are getting "real" letters.) The letters are mailed and their writers eagerly await their replies. Next week, in a faraway city, this process begins again as the teacher's friend takes her class through the same steps of learning to write letters.

The procedure just described is not difficult, but it does take time. Most classes would spend at least five 30- to 40-minute sessions going through the brainstorming, webbing, modeling, first draft writing, revising, and editing. The first time anything is done is always the hardest—for the teacher and the children. A month later, when the children have gotten their letters back and are ready to write again, the process will be much easier and will go much more quickly. After three or four letters, most children will know how to organize information and will write interesting and correctly formed letters with minimal help. By the end of the year, they will be expert letter writers and will have gained a lot of general writing skills in the process.

> Dear Ronald,
>
> I live in Clemmons, North Carolina. I have a new house, it is near the Yadkin River. The weather is getting warmer because it is Spring. In the summer it is hot here!
>
> I am seven years old. I am in second grade. My teacher's name is Mr. Dahler. He reads to us everyday and he is nice. My friends at school are Mitchell, Seth, and Bobby. We play soccer after school together. We are in a league. In the summer we swim together at the pool.
>
> Please write back and tell me about Chicago and your second grade class.
>
> Your friend,
> Ben

Reports—Focused Writing

Teachers often ask children to write reports. If the class is studying farm animals, friends, or famous African-Americans, the students are asked to choose one about which to write. **Teachers need to model how to write a report, not just assign one.** Reports are another form of focused writing in second or third grade.

Imagine that a class is doing a science unit on animals. The teacher has read aloud many animal books, and there are animal books on all different reading levels available during Self-Selected Reading. There are also encyclopedias and several computers in the classroom.

① Brainstorming

The teacher tells the class that they are going to take a week off from their individual writing to make a class book about animals. Together, they brainstorm the different animals about which they could write.

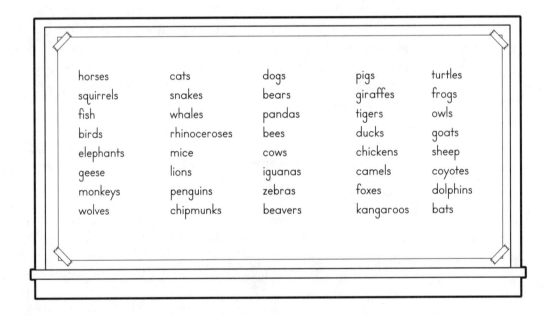

horses	cats	dogs	pigs	turtles
squirrels	snakes	bears	giraffes	frogs
fish	whales	pandas	tigers	owls
birds	rhinoceroses	bees	ducks	goats
elephants	mice	cows	chickens	sheep
geese	lions	iguanas	camels	coyotes
monkeys	penguins	zebras	foxes	dolphins
wolves	chipmunks	beavers	kangaroos	bats

❷ Narrowing the Topic

The teacher tells the children that each one of them will become an expert on one type of animal and write about it. Because she knows that some animals will be more popular than others, she asks them to write down the names of five animals they would like to do. She then assigns each child an animal on which to become an expert. The teacher chooses an animal no one else has chosen—pigs!

Things We Want to Find Out
Together, the teacher and the children come up with questions her report on pigs should answer.

The teacher writes each question on one large index card, and she labels another card, "Other Interesting Facts About Pigs."

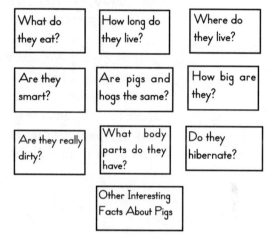

Next, the teacher gives the children large index cards and asks them to come up with questions about their animals. She helps them see that some of their questions (i.e., What do they eat? Where do they live?) might be just like hers, but that they should have questions specific to their animals, as well (i.e., Are pigs and hogs the same thing?). She also tells them that there will be other interesting facts about their animals that they should put on their "Other Interesting Facts" cards. The children begin to write their questions, and the teacher helps them.

❸ Read, Research, and Take Notes

For the next several days, the teacher gathers the children together and does her "research" on pigs. She puts the index cards in the pocket chart. She has written the questions as big as possible with a thick marker so that all the children can see them. As she reads about pigs from books and encyclopedias, the children stop her when they hear something that answers one of the questions or when they want to add a fact to the Interesting Facts card. She writes this information in smaller print on the cards. (It is important for children to be able to see the question so that they know where information will go, but they don't all need to see the notes about these questions.) The children and the teacher are amazed to learn that pigs are baby hogs, and that they can only really be called pigs until they are ten weeks old! The teacher reads and takes notes on pigs for about 15 minutes.

Then, the children take their cards to a spot where they can spread them out and do research on their animals. The teacher moves around the room and helps them as they record facts on their cards.

4 **Writing the Report**
After several days of note-taking, the teacher and the children are ready to begin writing their reports. The teacher models how she decides which information to include in each paragraph. Next, the children begin their reports and the teacher helps them decide how to organize their notes. When all the first drafts are written, children work with partners to revise and edit them. The teacher does a final edit, and the reports are typed on the computer, illustrated, and bound into a class book.

Just as for the focused writing lesson on letter writing, the first report writing focused lesson takes a lot of time and effort. In a month or so, however, when the class works together to do "biographies" of famous Americans, the process goes much more quickly, and the learning that took place during the first lesson becomes obvious. By participating in several focused report-writing lessons, all children learn how to write an informational article without copying from a book.

MAKING THE WRITING BLOCK MULTILEVEL

Writing is already a multilevel block because it is not limited by the availability or acceptability of appropriate books. If teachers allow children to choose their own topics, accept whatever level of first-draft writing each child can accomplish, and allow children to work on their pieces as many days as needed, all children can succeed in writing.

One of the major tenets of process writing is that children should choose their own topics. When children decide what they will write, they write about something of particular interest to them and consequently something that they know about. This may seem like belaboring the obvious, but it is a crucial component in making the writing process multilevel. When everyone writes about the same topic, the different levels of children's knowledge and writing ability become painfully obvious. **If students write about topics which interest them, they are more likely to succeed, as in this example:**

In one classroom, two boys each took a turn in the Author's Chair on the same day. Todd, a very advanced writer, read a book he had authored, titled "Rocks." His 16-page book contained illustrations and detailed descriptions of metamorphic, igneous, and sedimentary rocks. The next author was Joey, one of the struggling readers and writers in the classroom. He proudly read his eight-page illustrated book, titled "My New Bike." When the two boys read, the difference in their literacy levels was striking.

Later, several of the other children in the class were individually asked what they liked about the two pieces, and how they were different. The children replied, "Todd wrote about rocks, and Joey wrote about his bike." Opinions about the pieces were divided, but most children seemed to prefer the bike piece to the rock piece—bikes being of greater interest than rocks to most children!

Writing is multilevel when children choose their topics and write about what they know. The differences in the writing levels of children are obvious to adults, but children tend to focus on the topic and not notice the different writing levels.

Writing is also multilevel because, for some children, writing is the best avenue to becoming readers. When children who are struggling with reading write about their own experiences, and then read it back (even if no one else can read it!), they are using their own language and experiences to become readers. Often these children, who struggle with even the simplest material during Guided Reading, can read everything in their writing notebooks or folders. When children are writing, some of them are really working on becoming better writers; others are engaging in the same activity but, for them, writing is how they figure out reading.

In addition to teacher acceptance, children choosing their own topics, and teachers not expecting finished pieces each day, the Writing Block includes two teaching opportunities which promote the multilevel function of process writing: mini-lessons and conferences.

In mini-lessons, the teacher writes and the children get to watch her thinking as she writes. In these daily short lessons, teachers show all aspects of the writing process. They model topic selection, planning, writing, revising, and editing. They also write on a variety of topics in a variety of different forms. Some days they write short pieces. Other days, they work on pieces that take several days to complete. When doing longer pieces, they model how to reread previous writing in order to pick up the train of thought and continue writing.

Mini-lessons contribute to making writing multilevel when:

- **All different facets of the writing process are included.**

- **The teacher writes on a variety of topics in a variety of forms.**

- **The teacher intentionally writes some shorter, easier pieces and some more involved, longer pieces.**

Another opportunity for meeting the various needs and levels of children comes in the writing conference. In some classrooms, as students develop in their writing, children do some peer revising and editing and then come to the teacher ("editor-in-chief") for final revisions before publishing. By helping the children publish the their work, teachers have the opportunity to truly individualize their teaching. Looking at the child's writing usually reveals both what the child needs in order to move forward and what the child is ready to understand. The writing conference provides the "teachable moment" in which both advanced and struggling writers can be nudged forward in their literacy development.

Another way in which teachers assure that the Writing Block is a successful experience for all levels of writers is to spend a minute or two with a struggling reader before that child shares his work in the Author's Chair. If the child wants to share from a first-draft piece but is unable to read it, and if the teacher can't read it either, the teacher will coach the child to "tell" his piece rather than try to read it. If a struggling reader is about to read from a published piece for which the teacher has provided a lot of help, the teacher will practice read it with the child a time or two to assure that he can read it fluently when he is in the Author's Chair.

Kids' Comments about Writing:

"My favorite block is Writing because I like to write long, funny stories! And I like to illustrate and publish books."

"My favorite is Writing because you write about something you want to write about. And when it's your table's day, you get to share. When you finish, you can put it in a book."

"I like Writing because you can write any story you want."

"I like Writing because I like conferences, and I love to write."

"I like Writing best because I like making up my own stories. And because I like writing good make-believe and true stories."

The pages at the end of this chapter will provide you with a summary and review of information. There is an example of how one week in this block might look. Finally, there is a checklist many teachers use when they begin implementing this framework.

SUMMARY OF THE WRITING BLOCK

The purpose of this block is for students to see writing as a way to tell about things, to build fluency in writing, to learn to read through writing, to apply grammar and mechanics in writing, to learn particular forms of writing, and to maintain the self-confidence and motivation of struggling writers.

Total Time: 30-40 minutes

10 min.

Segment One: Mini-Lesson—Teacher Writing

The teacher presents a mini-lesson in which she models real writing and a skill or strategy. The mini-lesson has these elements:

- The mini-lesson focuses on writing, adding to, or editing a piece.

- The teacher refers to the Word Wall and other places in the room to model how words available in the room can help with spelling.

- The teacher models the use of an Editor's Checklist to promote and guide self-checking, peer revision, and editing. This checklist grows as appropriate expectations are added throughout the year.

20 min.

Segment Two: Children Writing and Conferencing

1. Students write on self-generated topics, individually paced at various stages of the writing process, perhaps working for multiple days on one piece.

2. Individual conferences occur between some students and the teacher while the other students write. Each student picks one piece, from three to five good first drafts, to revise, edit, and publish during the conference.

10 min.

Segment Three: Sharing

1. Selected students share briefly in the Author's Chair (approximately two minutes each) something they have written.

2. The "author" answers several questions from classmates about the writing. The teacher models the types of thoughtful questions students should learn to ask

Adapted from Implementing the Four-Blocks® Literacy Model by Cheryl Mahaffey Sigmon

A TYPICAL WEEK IN THE WRITING BLOCK

Monday

Segment 1: Mini-Lesson on Combining Sentences

1. The teacher calls the students to sit on the carpet around the overhead. She brainstorms aloud about what she might write: "I could tell you about what I did this weekend, or I could tell you about the new trick my puppy has learned. When we were starting our unit on travel this morning, I began to think about the very first plane trip I ever took. I think that's what I really want to write about today!"

2. She begins to write on a lined transparency. Occasionally she comes to a word that she has to "stretch out" by the way it sounds. She continues to compose a story about her very first airplane trip.

3. When she has finished her draft, she reads it aloud to the students. Then, she says, "When I was reading my piece aloud, I noticed that I used some short, choppy sentences. I am going to combine some of these sentences to make them a little more interesting. Watch as I try that with these two sentences."

4. The teacher makes the changes and then rereads the piece. She says that she likes it much better.

5. The students help her edit her piece using the Editor's Checklist.

6. The teacher dismisses the students to do their own writing: "Everyone who is starting a new piece can go back to your seat and get started. Everyone who is adding on to a piece can go back and continue writing. Those of you who are ready to revise and edit can go back to your seats and begin. Those of you who are publishing can go the publishing table. I need Tammy to come with me and finish the editing we started yesterday. Bernard will be next after Tammy finishes."

Segment 2

The students work at different stages of their writing while the teacher has brief conferences with the students who are ready to publish. When the timer sounds, the children put away their work and come to the sharing area to hear what their classmates have written.

Segment 3

The Monday students take turns in the Author's Chair. After each student reads, a couple of classmates comment on what they like and ask questions. Occasionally, the teacher models the kind of thoughtful questions that will help children think about their writing.

Tuesday

Segment 1: Mini-Lesson on Writing Postcards

1. The teacher calls the students to sit around the overhead projector and says, "Today in the Self-Selected Reading Block, we read Lynn Cherry's story called *The Armadillo from Amarillo* (Gulliver Books, 1994). The story had lots of pictures of postcards in it. I have several postcards here that friends and family members have mailed to me. Let's see where they've been and what they've seen. My sister Rebecca went to Anaheim, California, and saw the Pacific Ocean. My friend Anne sent this to me from New Orleans, Louisiana, where she saw the Mississippi River."

2. Next she says, "Today, I'm going to show you how to write a postcard. With so little space, you have to be brief. If you're traveling, you want to tell something about what you've seen and done."

3. The teacher draws the outline of a postcard on the overhead transparency and talks about where information goes. Then, she writes a sample card as though she were still on the vacation she took last summer.

4. After the teacher finishes the card, the children help her edit it using the Editor's Checklist. She tells the class that she has made some blank postcards and that they can use them this week if they would like to write postcards during their writing time.

Segment 2

Students work at different stages of their writing while the teacher has brief conferences.

Segment 3

The Tuesday children share in the Author's Chair.

Wednesday

Segment 1: Mini-Lesson on Run-On Sentences

1. The teacher calls the students to sit around the overhead projector. She brainstorms about what she will write that day.

2. After several ideas, she finally decides that she will write about her puppy, Tinker, and his latest adventure. She begins to write about her puppy digging out from under the fence and how she had to search for him.

3. After the teacher finishes her story, she rereads it and says, "The same thing happened in my story that sometimes happens in your stories. I have written a sentence that goes on and on. We call this a run-on sentence. I think I'll fix it."

4. She changes the run-on sentence into two good sentences. Next, she and the students use the Editor's Checklist to edit her piece.

Segment 2
Students work at different stages of their writing while the teacher has brief conferences.

Segment 3
The Wednesday children share in the Author's Chair.

Thursday
Segment 1: Mini-Lesson on Writing a Summary
1. The teacher calls the students to sit around the overhead projector. She brings with her a chart that the class made yesterday after talking about travel. The chart is a class-generated list of manners for people to observe when they are visiting someone's house. They have also read a book in Self-Selected Reading called *I Can't Take You Anywhere* by Phyllis Reynolds Naylor (Atheneum, 1997).

2. The teacher says she will use the chart to write a summary about manners. Then, she begins to show students how to organize the ideas into a summary. She writes a lead paragraph and another good paragraph and says, "I'll need to continue this tomorrow and write about some of the other important rules."

Segment 2
Students work at different stages of their writing while the teacher has brief conferences.

Segment 3
The Thursday children share in the Author's Chair.

Friday

Segment 1: Mini Lesson on Writing a Summary, Continued

The teacher calls the students to sit around the overhead projector. She reminds them that she needs to continue the summary that she started on Thursday. She reads over her lead paragraph and her second paragraph. Then, she adds another paragraph and a good ending. Finally, the class helps her edit the piece, using the Editor's Checklist.

Segment 2

Students work at different stages of their writing while the teacher has brief conferences.

Segment 3

The Friday children share in the Author's Chair.

Segment 3
The Friday children share in the Author's Chair.

TEACHER'S CHECKLIST FOR THE WRITING BLOCK

In preparing and presenting my lessons in this block, I have...

_____ 1. Selected a skill or strategy to introduce in my mini-lesson that is necessary to improve my students' writing.

_____ 2. Provided a good model of writing, though not so sophisticated that students feel they cannot attain a similarly good piece of writing.

_____ 3. Modeled adding on to a piece of writing by occasionally beginning a piece one day and continuing to write it the next day.

_____ 4. Chosen a piece of my own writing occasionally to have students help me revise.

_____ 5. Modeled the use of resources in the classroom for spelling when writing, such as Word Wall, charts, pictures, and theme boards.

_____ 6. Modeled how a student might "stretch-out" a word to figure out a temporary spelling.

_____ 7. Varied the topic, purpose, and audience of my mini-lessons on different days.

_____ 8. Encouraged students to write on their own topics.

_____ 9. Modeled during Author's Chair the types of higher-level questions about writing that students should ask of themselves and their peers.

_____ 10. Provided motivation for writing through several avenues of publishing, such as making a book, displaying work in the classroom or halls, or sharing via electronic mail with another class.

_____ 11. Developed an Editor's Checklist to assist students with self- and peer-editing of their work. This list grows appropriately as children develop in their writing.

_____ 12. Included some focused writing weeks to teach particular types of writing in Grades 2 and 3.

The fascinating world of words gives young learners the power to decode and comprehend as they read and the ability to spell and express their thoughts as they write. In Making Words, when children touch and manipulate letters, words magically appear, and patterns and relationships are revealed. Excitement builds as children apply cross checking strategies in Guess the Covered Word. Using Words You Know and Rounding Up the Rhymes help spelling become much more than the percentage of words correctly spelled on Friday and forgotten by Monday.

In Word Wall practice, decoding and spelling abilities are enhanced as children chant, write, and check words. Invented spelling remains developmentally appropriate for new words and works in progress. Word Wall words provide the correct spelling for the high-frequency words students use often in their writing.

Through the activities in the Working with Words Block, teachers can assess, monitor, and plan for the needs of the entire group, as well as the individual students. This ensures students learn the high-frequency words and engage in activities to learn how words work.

THE WORKING WITH WORDS BLOCK

Goals:

- **Learn to read and spell high-frequency words.**
- **Learn patterns used to decode and spell lots of other words.**
- **Transfer word knowledge to their own reading and writing.**

30 min.

In the Working with Words Block, children learn to read and spell high-frequency words and the patterns that allow them to decode and spell lots of other words. In this chapter, we will describe the activities in the Working with Words Block. Of course, these activities vary greatly depending on the grade level and the time of the year. For more detailed Working with Words Block activities by grade level, see *Month-by-Month Phonics for First Grade* (Cunningham & Hall, 1997), *Month-by-Month Phonics for Second Grade* (Hall & Cunningham 1998), and *Month-by-Month Phonics for Third Grade* (Cunningham & Hall, 1998).

WORD WALLS

Doing a Word Wall

The first ten minutes of this block are given to "doing" the Word Wall words. Doing a Word Wall is not the same thing as having a Word Wall. Having a Word Wall might mean putting all these words up somewhere in the room and telling students to use them. In many cases, struggling readers can't use them because they don't know them, and don't know which word is which!

10 min.

Teachers who *do* Word Walls (rather than just have Word Walls) report that *all* their children can learn these critical words. Here is the procedure:

Each week, the teacher selects five words and adds them to a wall or bulletin board in the room. The Word Wall grows as the year progresses. The words on the Word Wall are written on different colors of paper with a thick, black, permanent marker. Words are placed on the wall alphabetically by first letter and the first words added are very different from one another. When confusing words are added, they are put on different colored paper from the words with which they are usually confused.

Doing a Word Wall means:

- **Adding words gradually** (five a week).

- **Making words very accessible** by putting them where every student can see them, writing them in big black letters, and using a variety of colors so that the most often-confused words (for, from; that, them, they, this; etc.) are different colors.

- **Being selective and "stingy" about what words go on the wall**, limiting additions to those really common words which children use a lot in writing.

- **Practicing the words by chanting and writing them**, because struggling readers are not usually good visual learners and can't just look at and remember words.

- **Doing a variety of review activities** to provide enough practice so that the words are read and spelled instantly and automatically.

- **Making sure that Word Wall words are spelled correctly in any writing students do.**

Most teachers add five new words each week and **do at least one daily activity in which the children find, write, and chant the spelling of the words**. The activity takes longer on the day that words are added because it is necessary to take time to make sure that students associate meanings with the words and point out how the words are different from words with which they are often confused.

To begin the Word Wall practice, students number a sheet of paper from one to five. The teacher calls out five words, pointing to each and using it in a sentence. **As the teacher calls out each word, all the children clap and chant its spelling before writing it.** When all five words have been written, the teacher writes the words as students check and fix their own papers. **Many teachers include handwriting instruction with the daily Word Wall activity** and have children trace around the words to check the proper position of the letters.

On the day new words are added, the new words are called out, clapped, chanted, and written. The week's new words are often reviewed on the second day. During the rest of the week, however, any five words from the wall can be called out. Words with which children need much practice should be called out almost every day.

On-the-Back Word Wall Activities

Early in the year, it takes the whole ten minutes to call out, ch
five words. As the year goes on, however, and writing and co
come more fluent and automatic, the five words can usually b
utes. This leaves five minutes to do an *On-the-Back* activity wh
knowledge of the Word Wall words or helps them learn to spe

On-the-Back Endings

This activity helps children learn to spell Word Wall words which need an ending.
Imagine that these were the five Word Wall words you called out for children to
locate, cheer for, and write:

want	**eat**	**look**	**talk**	**play**

Have children turn over their papers. Say something like this:

> Today we are going to work on how to spell these Word Wall words when
> they need an ending. I will say some sentences like the ones many of you
> write, and you listen for the Word Wall word that has had an ending added:
>
> - My friends and I love **eating** at McDonald's®.
>
> - We were **looking** for some new shoes.
>
> - I was **talking** on the phone to my cousin.
>
> - My mom **wants** the new baby to be a girl.
>
> - My friend spent the night, and we **played** Nintendo® until 11:00.

After each sentence, the children identify the Word Wall word and the ending, decide how to spell the word, and write the word with the ending on their papers.

The example on the previous page uses three endings, **s**, **ed**, and **ing**, and five different words. **When first doing this activity, use fewer endings and/or fewer words.** For example, call out five words to write on the front, but concentrate on adding endings to only one or two of these on the back. Imagine that **eat** and **look** are two of the five words. These could be the sentences for the *On-the-Back* activity:

* He **looks** hungry.

* We were **looking** for Tommy.

* She **looked** in the closet.

* He **eats** peanut butter sandwiches every day.

* We were **eating** when the fire alarm went off.

The children would have the words **looks**, **looking**, **looked**, **eats**, and **eating** written on the backs of their papers.

These endings do not require any spelling changes. Later in the year, include some words that need to have the **e** dropped, a **y** changed to **i**, or a letter doubled. In second and third grade, in addition to **s**, **ed**, and **ing**, use sentences containing Word Wall words to which **y**, **ly**, **er**, and **est** have been added. Since we decide before writing each word how we will spell it, everyone spells each word correctly. This additional information about how to spell words with a variety of endings and spelling changes really moves the accelerated learners along in their writing ability.

On-the-Back Rhymes

Another popular *On-the-Back* activity helps children see how some Word Wall words can help them spell lots of other words that rhyme. **In many classrooms, teachers underline the spelling patterns and put stars or stickers on Word Wall words that have lots of other words with the same pattern.** On some days, the five words they call out for children to write on the front of their papers are all starred/stickered words.

For the *On-the-Back* activity, the teacher says a sentence which contains a word that rhymes with one of the day's words and is spelled with the same pattern. Children must decide which word rhymes and how to spell it. Imagine, for example, that these are the five words written on the front:

| school | ride | saw | car | best |

The children turn over their papers and the teacher asks them to listen to the following sentence for the word that rhymes with one of the words on the front:

Sometimes, my little sister is a pest.

The children decide that **pest** rhymes with **best** and they write **pest** next to number 1 on the backs of their papers.

The teacher continues to say sentences which children might actually use in their writing, such as these:

- I like to eat cole **slaw**.

- I went to a wedding because the **bride** is my cousin.

- Christmas is still very **far** away.

- I go to the YMCA and swim in the **pool**.

For each sentence, students decide which word rhymes with one of the words written on the front and use the spelling pattern to spell it.

Ally
1. school
2. ride
3. saw
4. car
5. best

Front

1. pest
2. slaw
3. bride
4. far
5. pool

On-the-Back

For an easier lesson, the teacher may use only one of the words written on the front as the rhyming match. Imagine that one of the words she has called out is **ride**. She could say sentences such as these:

> - I like to play **hide** and seek.
>
> - My cousin was the **bride**.
>
> - I picked Carl to be on my **side**.
>
> - We got a lot of clams at low **tide**.
>
> - I broke my arm when I fell off the **slide**.

When doing rhyming *On-the-Back* activities, the teacher comes up with the rhyming words and puts them in sentences similar to what children might actually write. She doesn't ask students for rhyming words because there are often—particularly with the long vowels—two spelling patterns. If she asked for words that rhymed with **ride**, the children might come up with **tried** and **cried**. It is important for children to learn about the two patterns, but first they must learn that we spell by pattern—not one letter for one sound.

On-the-Back Cross Checking

To practice Cross Checking, call out several words that begin with the same letter for students to write on the front, such as these:

went	want	was	what	where

Tell students that they will have to decide which word from the front makes sense in each sentence. Then, say a sentence leaving out one of the words. Students decide which word makes sense in your sentence and write that word. Here are some possible sentences with one of the above words left out:

> - I _____ to the beach.
>
> - It _____ very hot.
>
> - _____ do you want for lunch?
>
> - _____ should we go first?
>
> - I _____ to go home.

Be a Mind Reader

Be a Mind Reader is a favorite *On-the-Back* activity. **In this game, the teacher thinks of a word on the wall and then gives five clues about that word.**

The teacher has students number their papers from 1 to 5 and tells them that he is going to see who can read his mind and figure out which of the words on the board he is thinking of. The teacher tells the students he will give them five clues. By the fifth clue, everyone should guess the word, but if they read his mind they might get it before the fifth clue. For the first clue, the teacher always gives the same clue:

It's one of the words on the wall.

Students should write next to number 1 the word they think it might be. Each succeeding clue should narrow down what the word might be until, by clue five, there is only one possible word.

As the teacher gives clues, students write the word they believe it is next to each number on their paper. If succeeding clues confirm the word a student has written next to one number, then that student writes the same word next to the following number. Clues may include any features of the word the teacher wants students to notice (i.e., "It has more than two letters. It has less than four letters. It has an **e**. It does not have a **t**."). After clue five, the teacher says, "I know you all have the word next to number five, but who has it next to number 4? 3? 2? 1?"

Some students will have read your mind and will be as pleased as punch with themselves!

Be a Mind Reader Example:

1. It's one of the words on the wall.

2. It has four letters.

3. It begins with **w-h**.

4. The vowel is an **e**.

5. It begins the sentence: _____ will lunch be ready?

Word Wall Variations Across Grade Levels

During the daily Working with Words Block, children spend the first ten minutes practicing Word Wall words. Each day, the teacher calls out five words for which the children clap and cheer (in a rhythmic fashion), write, and then check. The students also focus on the handwriting of the words as they check them. What varies from grade to grade is the words.

First Grade

Most first-grade teachers begin their Word Walls with the names of the children, adding one each day rather than five on Monday. When doing the names of the children, they clap and cheer them, but they don't usually write them, because children's writing abilities are limited and instruction on letter formation is just beginning. Once the names of the children are there, high-frequency words are added, five per week. At this point, they usually begin writing the words.

First-grade teachers usually choose words from Guided Reading selections to add to the wall. Because Word Wall words are high-frequency words, they will occur in the selections children are reading. Teachers consult a high-frequency list and then add the most frequent ones from anything read during Guided Reading. There is no particular order in which to add the words, but teachers should try not to add two in the same week that begin with the same letter. They should also try to include some easier words (me, go, in) along with some of the trickier ones (what, friend, there). Many teachers add *what*, *do*, *you*, *see*, and *at* after reading *Brown Bear, Brown Bear, What Do You See?* by Bill Martin, Jr. (Holt, Rinehart, Winston, 1967).

In addition to high-frequency words, many first-grade teachers like to have a word on the wall to represent each of the beginning sounds, along with **sh**, **ch**, **th**, and **wh**.

partial Word Wall shown (Carson-Dellosa's Word Wall "Plus" for First Grade CD-2501)

First-Grade Word Wall List

Below is a list of words that a Word Wall might contain at the end of first grade. This one includes high-frequency words, a few frequently-written-by-first-graders words (such as **favorite**, **sister**, and **brother**), and examples for all beginning sounds. Starred words have a spelling pattern and will help children spell lots of rhyming words.

after	he	said
all*	her	saw*
am*	here	school*
and*	him*	see*
animal	his	she
are	house	sister
at*	how*	some
be	I	talk*
best*	in*	teacher
because	is	tell*
big*	it*	that*
boy*	jump*	the
brother	kick*	them
but*	like*	there
can*	little	they
can't	look*	thing*
car*	made*	this
children	make*	to
come	me	up
day*	my*	us
did*	new*	very
do	nice*	want
down*	night*	was
eat*	no	we
favorite	not*	went*
for	of	what
friend	off	when*
from	old*	where
fun*	on	who
get	out*	why*
girl	over	will*
give	people	with
go	play*	won't
good	pretty	you
had*	quit*	your
has	rain*	zoo
have	ride*	

Second Grade

In second grade, word selection is based more on what the teacher observes in children's writing than on what words they have read during Guided Reading. The emphasis is still on high-frequency words, but the teacher selects those that are irregularly spelled, particularly those misspelled in students' first-draft writing.

Many second-grade teachers begin their Word Walls with the words *they,* *said,* *was,* *have,* **and** *because*—**words most second graders can read but cannot spell.** They do not put high-frequency words that are easy to spell on a second grade Word Wall unless they have second graders who still cannot spell **me**, **in**, **go**, etc. Hard-to-spell, high-frequency words are often on the first-grade Word Wall and then put back again on the second-grade Word Wall. In schools in which children have had a Word Wall in first grade, they often know which words are hard for them to spell and ask to have these words put back on their second-grade Word Wall.

Once the hard-to-spell, high-frequency words are on the wall, the teacher should try to include the following:

- An example word for each letter combination, including **ch**, **sh**, **th**, **wh**, **qu**, **ph**, **wr**, and **kn**.

- Examples for the less common **c** and **g** sounds.

- Words representing the most common blends: **bl**, **br**, **cl**, **cr**, **dr**, **fl**, **fr**, **gr**, **pl**, **pr**, **sk**, **sl**, **sm**, **sn**, **sp**, **st**, and **tr**.

- Examples for the most common vowel patterns:
  cr<u>a</u>sh, **m<u>a</u>ke**, **r<u>ai</u>n**, **pl<u>aye</u>d**, **c<u>ar</u>**, **s<u>aw</u>**, **c<u>augh</u>t**
  w<u>e</u>nt, **<u>ea</u>t**, **gr<u>ee</u>n**, **sist<u>er</u>**, **n<u>ew</u>**
  <u>i</u>nto, **r<u>i</u>de**, **r<u>igh</u>t**, **g<u>ir</u>l**, **th<u>i</u>ng**
  n<u>o</u>t, **th<u>ose</u>**, **fl<u>oa</u>t**, **<u>or</u>**, **<u>ou</u>tside**, **b<u>oy</u>**, **sh<u>ook</u>**, **sch<u>ool</u>**, **h<u>ow</u>**, **sl<u>ow</u>**,
  b<u>u</u>g, **<u>use</u>**, **h<u>ur</u>t**
  wh<u>y</u>, **ver<u>y</u>**

- The most commonly written contractions: **can't, didn't, don't, it's, that's, they're, won't.**

- Homophones: **to, too, two; there, their, they're; right, write; one, won; new, knew.**

- Example words with **s**, **ed**, and **ing**.

kind
away
check
sister
that's
light
laugh
together
after
beautiful
because
city
other
really

Second-Grade Word Wall List

Below is a list of words that a Word Wall might contain at the end of second grade. (Some of these words are also on the first-grade Word Wall because it takes some children two years to learn to spell these automatically every time they write.) Starred words have spelling patterns that help spell lots of rhyming words. Clues (shown in parentheses below) are put next to all but one of the homophones.

about	into	slow*
after	it's	small*
again	joke*	snap*
are	jump*	sometimes
beautiful	junk*	sports*
because	kicked*	stop*
before	knew*	tell*
best*	line*	than*
black*	little	thank*
boy*	made*	that's
brothers	mail*	their
bug*	make*	them
can't	many	then*
car*	more*	there (here)
caught	name*	they
children	new* (old)	they're (they are)
city	nice*	thing*
clock*	not*	those
could	off	to
crash*	one (1)	too (Too late!)
crashes	or	trip*
didn't	other	truck*
don't	our	two (2)
drink*	outside	use
eating*	people	very
every	phone*	wanted
favorite	played*	was
first	pretty	went*
float*	quit*	were
found*	rain*	what
friends	really	when*
girl	ride*	where
green	right* (Wrong!)	who
gym	said	why*
have	sale*	will*
here	saw*	with
house	school*	won
how*	shook*	won't
hurt	sister	write*
I	skate*	writing

Third Grade

Third-grade teachers often ask if they need a Word Wall (often phrased as "I don't need a Word Wall, do I?"). They can answer that question for themselves by looking at the first-draft writing of their children.

You need a Word Wall in third grade if you find that many children misspell common, non-pattern-following words such as these:

they	could	does	people	from
were	where	said	because	again

You also need to look at how your children are spelling common homophones such as these:

to, too, two   their, there, they're   no, know

110 Third Grade Word Wall Words

The 110 words on the next page are suggested words for use on the Word Wall during third grade. The list contains the following:

- the most frequently misspelled words at third-grade level, such as **because**, **they**, **enough**, and **laughed**.

- the most commonly confused homophones, such as **to/too/two**, **write/right**, and **they're/there/their**.

- the most common contractions, such as **they're**, **can't**, **wouldn't**, **I'm**, and **it's**.

- the most common compound words, such as **everybody**, **everything**, **sometimes**, **into**, and **something**.

- a word beginning with each letter, including examples for the s sound of **c** (**city**) and the **j** sound of **g** (**general**).

- examples for the common endings and suffixes (**s**, **es**, **ed**, **ing**, **ly**, **er**, **or**, **ful**, **less**, **ness**, **en**, **able**, **ible**, **tion**, **sion**) with common spelling changes (drop **e**, change **y** to **i**, double the final consonant). Examples include **probably**, **especially**, **visually**, **friendly**, **hopeless**, and **laughed**.

- examples for the most common prefixes: **un**, **re**, **dis**, **im**, **in** (i.e., **discover**, **recycle**, **impossible**, **unhappiness**, **independent**).

partial Word Wall shown (Carson-Dellosa's Word Wall "Plus" for Third Grade CD-2504)

Third-Grade Word Wall List

Below is a list of words that a Word Wall might contain at the end of third grade. A clue (opposite word, picture, etc.) is attached to all but one of the homophones so that children can tell which one is which. (If many of your third-grade students are not using blends and rhyming patterns to spell words while writing, you may need to use the second-grade list. In third grade, the decisions about what words you need can only be made by looking at how children spell words in their first-draft writing.)

about	hole	there (here)
again	hopeless	they
almost	I'm	they're (they are)
also	impossible	thought
always	independent	threw (ball picture)
another	into	through
anyone	it's (it is)	to
are	its	too (too late!)
beautiful	journal	trouble
because	knew	two (2)
before	know	unhappiness
buy	laughed	until
by	let's	usually
can't	lovable	vacation
city	myself	very
could	new (old)	want
community	no (yes)	was
confusion	off	wear (t-shirt picture)
countries	one	weather (weather picture)
didn't	our	we're (we are)
discover	people	went
doesn't	pretty	were
don't	prettier	what
enough	prettiest	when
especially	probably	where
everybody	question	whether
everything	really	who
except	recycle	whole
exciting	right	winner
favorite	said	with
first	school	won
friendly	something	won't
getting	sometimes	wouldn't
general	terrible	write
governor	that's	your
have	their	you're (you are)
hidden	then	

PHONICS AND SPELLING

Teaching children phonics is a lot easier than teaching children to use the phonics they know. When phonics is taught in a way that is removed from reading and writing, children often learn what letters make what sounds but are unable to quickly apply this knowledge to an unfamiliar word in their reading or writing. **English is not a simple language to learn to decode and spell. Many of the consonants and all the vowels have a variety of sounds, depending on the surrounding letters.** Vowels do not have just short and long sounds.

This can be clearly understood by looking at any sentence and thinking about what the vowels do in that sentence.

In the previous sentence, for example, these words contain the vowel **o**:

> **understood** **looking** **about** **vowels** **do**

None of these **o**'s represents the short or long sound of **o**.

In the same sentence, these words contain the vowel **e**:

> **be** **clearly** **understood** **sentence** **vowels**

The **e** in the word **be** represents the long **e** sound, and two of the three **e**'s in the sentence represent the short sound of **e**. The **e** represents different sounds, not short or long, in **clearly**, **understood**, and **vowels**.

There is logic to the sounds represented by letters in English, but the logic is in the pattern, not in simple "vowel rules."

Looking again at the words above containing **o**, we see that the two **o**'s in **understood** and **looking** have the same sound and we know that other **o-o-d** and **o-o-k** words, including **good, hood, cook,** and **shook,** share this sound. The **ou** in **about** has the same sound that it has in other **o-u-t** words, including **out, shout,** and **clout.** The **ow** in **vowels** has the same sound in words such as **now, how,** and **cow.** Only the **o** in **do** does not follow a predictable pattern.

If we look at the patterns in **clearly, understood,** and **vowels,** we see the **e-a-r** representing the same sound as it does in **ear, hear,** and **dear;** the **e-r** representing the same sound it does in **her, mother,** and **father;** and the **e-l** representing the same sound we hear in **towel, camel,** and **level.**

Phonics—the relationships between letters and sounds—makes sense in English, but only if you know to look for patterns of letters rather than individual letters. These patterns determine the sounds for consonant letters as well as vowels. Psychologists tell us that our brains separate unknown words into their onsets—all the letters up to the vowel—and the rimes—the vowel and letters following it. The first time we ever saw the words **spew**, **mite**, and **phrase**, we separated their onsets (**s-p**, **m**, **p-h-r**) from their rimes (**e-w**, **i-t-e**, **a-s-e**), and then used what we knew about consonant and vowel patterns to come up with sounds for each part and combine them. **To be good decoders and spellers, children need to learn to quickly separate words into these parts, think of sounds associated with the patterns, and recombine the sounds.**

After the daily Word Wall practice, the remaining 20-25 minutes of Working with Words time is given to an activity which helps children learn the onset and rime patterns and how to use them to decode and spell new words. A variety of activities are used. Five of the most popular activities will be described on the following pages.

- Rounding Up the Rhymes
- Making Words
- Guess the Covered Word
- Using Words You Know
- Reading/Writing Rhymes

20 min.

Rounding Up the Rhymes

Rounding Up the Rhymes is a Working with Words Block activity that follows the reading of a selection during Guided Reading (or a book the teacher has read aloud at the beginning of the Self-Selected Reading time) that has lots of rhyming words with the same spelling pattern.

Here is an example using *One Fish, Two Fish, Red Fish, Blue Fish* by Dr. Seuss (Random House, 1960). The first (and often second) reading of anything should be focused on meaning and enjoyment. *One Fish, Two Fish, Red Fish, Blue Fish*, like most other Dr. Seuss books, has delightful imaginary characters who engage in all kinds of funny antics—a lot to discuss and enjoy!

1 **Read the Book**

To do *Rounding Up the Rhymes*, **take the book out again during the Working with Words Block and reread several pages, focusing on the rhyming words**. Choose pages that have lots of rhymes with the same pattern so that children will see the connection between rhyming words and spelling pattern. For this example, begin with page 18, which features Mr. Gump on his seven-hump Wump and go through page 23, which features Mike with his three-people bike. As you read each page, **encourage the children to chime in and try to hear the rhymes they are saying**.

2 **Round Up the Rhymes**

As children tell the rhyming words, **write them on index cards and put them in a pocket chart**. Here are the rhyming pairs rounded up from these pages:

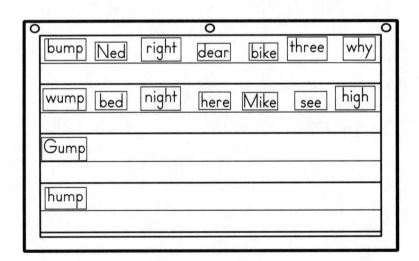

Next, **remind the children that words which rhyme usually have the same spelling pattern**. The children can then come and underline the spelling pattern in each set of rhymes and decide whether or not they are the same. Because you want rhymes with the same spelling pattern, discard **dear** and **here**: "**Dear** and **hear** do rhyme, but for the next part of this activity, we only want rhymes with the same spelling pattern. So we are going to throw these away."

Discard **why** and **high** for the same reasons. You now have five sets of words that rhyme and have the same spelling pattern in the pocket chart:

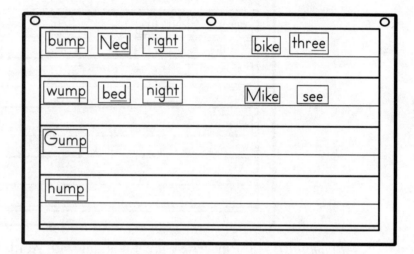

3 **Transfer**

The final part of this activity is to use these words to read and write some other words. **This is the transfer step, and it is critical to the success of this activity** for children who "only learn what we teach." The teacher begins the transfer part of this activity by telling children something like this:

"You know that when you are reading books and writing stories, there are many words you have never seen before. You have to figure them out. One way many people figure out how to read and spell new words is to see if they already know any rhyming words, or words that have the same spelling pattern. I am going to write some words, and you can see which words with the same spelling pattern will help you read them. Then, we are going to try to spell some words by deciding if they rhyme with any of the words in our pocket chart."

The teacher writes a word—**free**—that rhymes and has the same spelling pattern as some of the rounded-up rhymes. Without letting children pronounce the word, she has someone put it with the rhyming words that will help figure it out. Once **free** is placed under **three** and **see**, have the class pronounce all three words. Do this reading transfer with another word or two (**strike**, **stump**). Then, do the spelling transfer by saying a few words (**sped**, **bright**, **thump**), having students decide with which words they rhyme, and asking students to use the rhymes to spell them. At the end of the activity, the rounded-up rhymes, along with the transfer words, are lined up in the pocket chart.

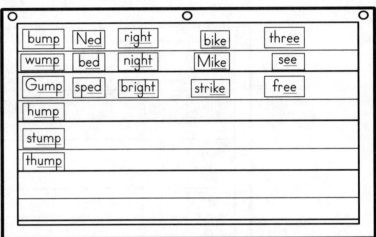

Rounding Up the Rhymes is a great Working with Words Block activity to follow the reading of any book which has several pages on which there are rhyming words with the same spelling pattern. **Having the rhymes come from a book and doing some transfer rhymes increases the probability that children will actually use rhyming words they know, as they encounter new words in their reading and need to spell words while writing.** *Rounding Up the Rhymes* is an appropriate activity to do when most children have developed the ability to hear rhymes and are ready to see how rhyming patterns work.

Other good books with lots of rhyming words include:

Golden Bear by Ruth Young (Scholastic, 1992).

House Mouse, Senate Mouse by Peter & Cheryl Barnes (Rosebud Books, 1996).

How I Spent My Summer Vacation by Mark Teague (Crown Publishers, 1995).

Inside, Outside Christmas by Robin Spowart (Holiday House, 1998).

The Monster Book of ABC Sounds by Alan Snow (Puffin Pied Piper Books, 1994).

My Nose Is a Hose by Kent Salisbury (McClanahan, 1997).

My Teacher, My Friend by P. K. Hallinan (Children's Press, 1989).

One Fish, Two Fish, Red Fish, Blue Fish by Dr. Seuss (Random House, 1960).

One Less Fish by Kim Michelle Toft and Allan Sheather (Charlesbridge, 1998).

Puffins Climb, Penguins Rhyme by Bruce McMillan (Harcourt Brace, 1995).

Saturday Night at the Dinosaur Stomp by Carol D. Sheilds (Scholastic, 1997).

This Is the Pumpkin by Abby Levine (Albert Whitman & Co., 1998).

This Is the Sea That Feeds Us by Robert Baldwen (Dawn, 1998).

Those Can Do Pigs by David McPhail (Scholastic, 1996).

Woodrow, the White House Mouse by Peter & Cheryl Barnes (Rosebud Books, 1995).

Zoo-Looking by Mem Fox (Mondo, 1996).

Making Words

Making Words **(Cunningham & Hall, 1994; Cunningham & Hall, 1997) is an active, hands-on, manipulative activity in which children learn how to look for patterns in words and how changing just one letter changes the whole word.** The children are given six to eight letters which will form a final "secret" word. The lesson begins with small words, builds to longer words, and finally ends with the "secret" word that can be made with all the letters. Then, students sort the words according to a variety of patterns, such as beginning sounds, endings, and rhymes. They transfer the patterns by using the words sorted to read and spell words with similar patterns.

For this example lesson, each child has five consonant cards, **d**, **p**, **r**, **s**, **s**, and two vowel cards, **e** and **i**. In the pocket chart at the front of the room, the teacher has large cards with the same seven letters. His cards, like the small letter cards used by the children, have the uppercase letter on one side and lowercase letter on the other side. The consonant letters are written in black and the two vowels are in red. (See page 147 for detailed steps in planning a *Making Words* lesson.)

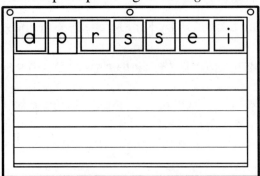

① Make Step

The teacher begins by making sure that each child has all the letters that are needed. "What two vowels will we use to make words today?" he asks. The children hold up the red **i** and **e** cards. The children then name the consonants. The teacher writes the number 3 on the board and says:

> "The first three-letter word I want you to make today is a word that you already know—**red**."

He sends someone who has quickly spelled **red** to the pocket chart to make **red** with the big letters, and to put an index card with the word **red** written on it in the chart. He then gives this direction:

> "Just change your vowel and you can change **red** into **rid**. Sometimes, I ask you to clean out your desks and get **rid** of the junk."

Next, he writes a 4 on the board and says, "Add just one letter to **rid** to make the four-letter word **ride**."

The lesson continues with the children making words with their individual letter cards, followed by a child going to the pocket chart to make the word and put the index card word in the pocket chart.

The teacher does not wait for everyone to make the word before sending someone to the pocket chart, and some children are still making their words as the word is being made with the pocket chart letters. Before making another word, the teacher reminds children to fix their words to match the one made with the big letters.

Directed by the teacher, the children change **ride** to **side**. Then, they do an "abracadabra" in which they just move around the letters in **side** to spell **dies**. They change the first letter in **dies** to spell **pies**.

The teacher writes a 5 on the board and says, "Add a letter to **pies** to spell **pries**. 'The boy **pries** open the top of the rusty old box.'"

Pries is changed to **dries** and then to **spies**. Then, the teacher gives this direction:

"Change just one letter to change **spies** to **spied**. 'She **spied** a quarter in a dusty corner.' Now, change **spied** to **pried**. 'It took a lot of work, but finally they **pried** the door open.'"

Next, the teacher tells children they can do another "abracadabra" and turn the **pried** that means "forced open" into the **pride** that he is always telling them they need to take in their work. They make two more five letter words, **dress** and **press**.

Finally, the teacher says, "I don't have any six-letter words for you today, so I am coming around to see who has the secret word."

He gives the children one minute, and several children have figured out the secret word, **spiders**. He sends one child to make **spiders** with the big letters and put the index card word **spiders** in the pocket chart.

② **Sort Step**

After making the words, it is time to sort for patterns, and then use those patterns to read and spell a few new words. The teacher has the children read all the words they have made, which are now displayed in the pocket chart:

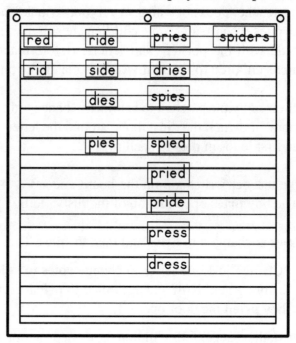

He then has children pull out and line up under one another the words that rhyme and have the same spelling pattern:

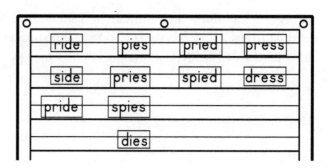

3 **Transfer Step**

The final step of every *Making Words* lesson is the transfer step. Once the rhymes are sorted, the teacher shows children an index card on which the word **chess** is written:

> "What if you were reading and came to this word and didn't know it? Don't say this word even if you know it. Who can go and put this word with the rhyming words that will help you figure it out?"

A child places **chess** under the other **e-s-s** words, and all the children pronounce **chess**. Next, the teacher says:

> "I have two more words you might not immediately know if you came to them in your reading."

He shows them cards on which he has written **glide** and **fried**. Children place these words under the rhyming words with the same patterns and pronounce them.

The teacher then explains that students can use rhyming patterns to help them in writing, too.

> "Thinking of words that rhyme helps you when you are trying to spell a word, too. What if you were writing and needed to spell **ties**? Which rhyming words would help you?"

The children decide that **ties** rhymes with **dies**, **pies**, **dries**, **pries**, and **spies** and would probably be spelled **t-i-e-s**.

The teacher helps the children notice the two spelling patterns, **ied** and **ide**, for the same rhyme:

> "When there are two spelling patterns for the same rhyme, we usually just have to pick the one that looks right, ask for help, or look in the dictionary to see which way to spell it. For these spelling patterns, though, there is a clue you can use if think about related words."

The teacher writes the words **spy**, **fry**, and **pry** next to **spied**, **fried**, and **pried**. The children talk about how the words are related and how **y** is changed to **i** when adding **ed**.

> "I am going to say a word that rhymes with **side**, **ride**, **pride**, and **slide**, and also with **spied**, **pried**, and **fried**. It could be spelled with either pattern, but if you think about its related word, you can probably figure it out. The word is **cried**. 'The baby **cried** all night.' How do you think you would spell **cried**?"

Several children's hands wave enthusiastically, and they are proud to explain that the word would be spelled **c-r-i-e-d** because the related word is **cry** and the **y** is changed to an **i**. (If your children are not at the stage where they could understand this **ide/ied** distinction and you want to do the spiders lesson, simply have them make two other words, such as **dip** and **drip**, instead of **spied** and **pried**.)

Homework Sheet

For homework, the children have the *Making Words* homework sheet. The letters **e**, **i**, **d**, **p**, **r**, **s**, and **s** are in boxes along the top and there are larger boxes below for children to write words. They cut the letters apart, write capitals on the backs, and then fill the boxes with words they can make, including some made in class and others they think of.

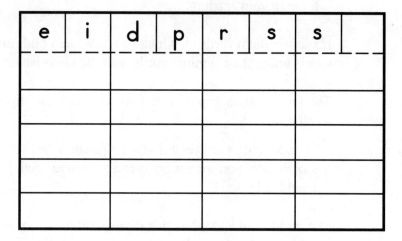

Several children comment when they bring back the sheets the next day that they showed their parents how words with both patterns, **ied** and **ide**, rhyme. They explained that they can figure out how to spell words if they think about related words like **cry** and **cried**. They then pointed out that it worked for **try/tried** and **dry/dried**, too. Their pride in their word wizardry is evident!

Steps in Planning a *Making Words* Lesson

1. Decide upon a "secret word" which can be made with all the letters. In choosing this word, consider child interest, the curriculum tie-ins you can make, and the letter/sound patterns to which you can draw children's attention through the sorting at the end.

2. Make a list of other words that can be made from these letters.

3. From all the words you could make, pick 12–15 words using these criteria:

   • Words that you can sort for the pattern you want to emphasize.

   • Little words and big words so that the lesson is a multilevel lesson (Making the little words helps your struggling students; making the big words challenges your highest-achieving students).

   • "Abracadabra" words that can be made with the same letters in different places (**side/dies**) so children are reminded that, when words are spelled, the order of the letters is crucial.

   • A proper name or two to remind students to use capital letters.

   • Words that most students have in their listening vocabularies.

4. Write all the words on index cards and order them from shortest to longest.

5. Once you have the two-letter, three-letter, etc., words together, order them so you can emphasize letter patterns and show how changing the position of the letters, changing one letter, or adding one letter results in a different word.

6. Choose some letters or patterns by which to sort.

7. Choose four transfer words—uncommon words you can read and spell based on the rhyming words.

8. Store the cards in an envelope. On the envelope, write the words in order, the patterns for which you will sort, and the transfer words.

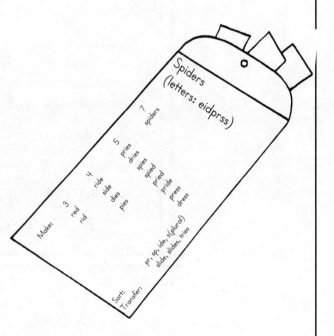

Spiders
(letters: eidprss)

7
spiders

5
pries
dries
spies
spied
pried
pride
press
dress

4
ride
side
dies
pies

3
red
rid

Make:

pr: sp: ide, s (plural)
slides, slides, tries

Sort:
Transfer:

Guess the covered word.

20 min.

Guess the Covered Word

Guess the Covered Word is another popular Working with Words Block activity. **Its purpose is to help children practice the important strategy of cross-checking meaning with letter-sound information.** Here is the procedure:

The teacher writes four or five sentences on the board, covering a word in each sentence with two sticky notes—one covering the onset, all the consonants prior to the first vowel, and the other sticky note covering the rest of the word. Most teachers tear their sticky notes so that children also become sensitive to word length.

The children read each sentence, then make several guesses for the covered word. (There are generally many possibilities for a word that will fit the context and the teacher points out that there are many possibilities when you can't see any of the letters.) The guesses are written on the board.

Next, the teacher takes off the first sticky note, which always covers all the letters up to the vowel.

Guesses which don't begin with these letters are erased and new guesses which both fit the meaning and start with the right beginning letters are made.

When all the guesses which fit both meaning and beginning sounds have been written, the whole word is revealed.

Pets

Juan might buy a pet turtle.

~~dog~~
~~rabbit~~ tarantula
turtle   tortoise

Joyce might buy a pet dachshund.

Kevin might buy a pet boa.

~~hamster~~
dog   dachshund
~~bird~~   boa
~~mongoose~~

Cassius might buy a p⬚⬚⬚.

Dottie might buy a pet ⬚⬚⬚.

~~chicken~~
dalmation

20 min.

Using Words You Know

There are hundreds of spelling patterns commonly found in one- and two-syllable words. **A good reader figures out new words by looking at the spelling pattern and thinking of other words with that pattern.** To spell a new word, a good reader thinks of a rhyming word and tries that pattern to see if it looks right. If it doesn't look right, he thinks of another word that rhymes, but has a different spelling pattern. *Using Words You Know* **is an activity to help children learn to use the many words they can read and spell to read and spell hundreds of other words.** Here is the procedure:

To plan a *Using Words You Know* lesson, pick three or four words your students know which have many rhyming words spelled the same way. You can use high-frequency words such as **big, play,** and **not.** You can also use color words, number words, vehicle words, food words, animal words, or seasonal words—any words your children know that have lots of rhyming words. For this example lesson, we will use the number words **ten, five,** and **nine.**

Using the board or overhead, make three columns and head them with the key words. Have each student do the same on a sheet of paper. Tell students that you will show them a word that rhymes with **ten, five,** or **nine.** When you show them the word, have them write it in the column under the rhyming word. Then, have them use the rhyming word to decode the new word. Have them verbalize the strategy they are using by saying something like, "If **t-e-n** is **ten, G-l-e-n** must be **Glen.**"

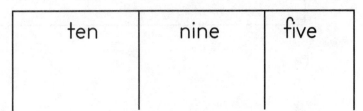

ten	nine	five

Write **Glen** under **ten** in your column and show them the next word. Do not let anyone say the word until they have written it in the correct column. Have them verbalize their strategy as they tell you the word: "If **f-i-v-e** is **five, d-r-i-v-e** is **drive.**"

After you have shown the children several words and they have used the known word to decode them, help them practice using known words to spell unknown words. This time, say a word, such as **shine,** and have students write **shine** under the word with which it rhymes. Have them verbalize how they spelled **shine** by leading them to explain, "If **nine** is spelled **n-i-n-e, shine** is probably spelled **s-h-i-n-e.**"

For these lessons, be sure that you tell the students what rhyming words to spell instead of having them come up with the words. In English, there are often two spelling patterns for the same rhyme. If you ask them what rhymes with **three**, they are apt to come up with words with the **e** pattern, such as **me** and **he**. So, for this strategy, you supply the words that rhyme and only choose rhymes with the same spelling pattern.

You can plan *Using Words You Know* lessons quickly and easily by using a rhyming dictionary. Here are some words that rhyme with and have the same spelling pattern as **ten**, **nine**, and **five**:

t<u>en</u>	n<u>ine</u>	f<u>ive</u>
Glen	shine	dive
wren	pine	drive
hen	spine	jive
men	fine	hive
then	line	strive
when	mine	
Ben	whine	
	vine	

20 min.

Reading/Writing Rhymes

Reading/Writing Rhymes **is an activity which gives students practice using patterns to decode and spell hundreds of words.** Once all the rhyming words are generated on a chart, students write rhymes using these words, and then read each other's rhymes. Because writing and reading are connected to every lesson, students learn how you use these patterns as you actually read and write. Here is an example of how one *Reading/Writing Rhymes* lesson might be carried out:

1 The teacher has distributed the whole set of beginning letter cards to the children. Because there are more onsets than children, most children have two cards. The cards (3" x 5" index cards) are laminated and have **single-letter consonant onsets written in blue, the blends in red, and the digraphs and other two-letter combinations in green**. On one side of each card, the first letter of the onset is a capital letter. In passing out the cards, the teacher has considered the levels of her children. Children who are still learning single initial consonants are given these. The most advanced children are given the less-common, more-complex onsets, such as **str** and **ph**.

The onset deck contains 50 beginning letter cards, including these:

Single consonants in blue:
b c d f g h j k l m n p r s t v w y z

Digraphs (two letters, one sound) in green: **sh ch wh th**

Other two-letter, one sound combinations in green: **ph wr kn qu**

Blends (beginning letters blended together, also called clusters) in red:
bl br cl cr dr fl fr gl gr pl pr sc scr sk sl sm sn sp spr st str sw tr

To make instruction as "non-jargony" as possible, refer to all these cards as beginning letters cards. Children learn that when they are trying to figure out how to read or spell a word, they should use all the letters up to the vowel. In the current climate, some schools demand that children learn the terminology. Terms such as consonants, blends, digraphs, clusters, etc., are confusing to many children and can actually interfere with their learning how to use letters and sounds. The terminology is included here. Do not use it with your students unless they will be penalized for not knowing it. **Regardless of what you call it, try to ensure that all your children learn that when trying to read or spell a new word, they should use all the letters up to the vowel "to do the first part" and then look at the spelling pattern—the rest of the word.**

Once all the onset cards are distributed, the teacher writes the spelling pattern with which the class is working eight times on a piece of chart paper. As she writes it each time, she has the children help spell it and pronounce it.

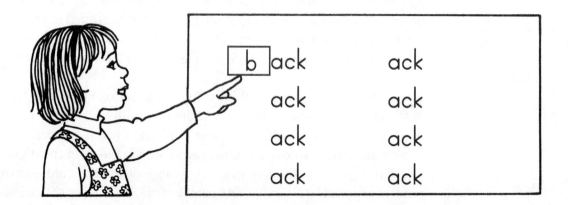

2 Next, the teacher invites children to come up who have cards that they think will make words. Then, they place the cards next to one of the written spelling patterns, and pronounce the word. If the word is indeed a real word, the teacher uses the word in a sentence and writes that word on the chart.** If the word is not a real word, she explains why she cannot write it on the chart. (If a word is a real word and does rhyme but has a different spelling pattern, such as **planned** to rhyme with **and**, explain that it rhymes but has a different pattern and include it on the bottom of the chart with an asterisk next to it.) The teacher writes names with capital letters and, if a word can be both a name and not a name, such as **Jack** and **jack**, she writes it both ways.

When all the children who think they can spell words by adding their beginning letters to the spelling pattern have had a turn, the teacher calls up children to make the words not yet on the chart. She says something like, "I think the person with the **wh** card could come up here and add **wh** to **ack** to make a word we know."

The teacher tries to include all the words that any of the children would have in their listening vocabulary but avoids really obscure words. If the eight patterns on the chart are made into complete words, she adds as many as needed. Finally, if the class can think of some good longer words that rhyme and have that spelling pattern, the teacher adds them. Of course, since the children don't have all the letters to spell these longer words, the teacher just writes these on the list.

_ack		
back	crack	whack
Jack	knack	backpack
quack	stack	fullback
track	snack	attack
sack	shack	hijack
Mack	tack	racetrack
pack	rack	
black	Zack	

3 Once the chart of rhyming words is written, the class works together in a shared writing format to write a silly rhyme using lots of the rhyming words.

The cop went to shop at the Stop and Shop for a mop.

4 Next, the children write rhymes of their own. Many teachers put them with small groups or partners to write these rhymes and then let different children read their rhymes to the class.

Don't stop or hop, but mop the drop so we can shop at the Stop and Shop and see if there is a new crop.

Clop, clop went the horse. Hop, hop went the rabbit. Stop, stop said the pop. I will drop my mop if you don't stop.

Jack and Mack ate a snack from his back pack. They packed the snack to eat at the black shack near the racetrack.

Zack went back to see Mr. Mack when he heard a quack near the track. There sat Jack with a backpack sitting on a crack with his snack.

When the class has made several charts, the teacher reviews with students all the rhyming words on all the charts and then lets students write rhymes using words from all the charts. Many teachers let each child pick one rhyme to edit and illustrate, then compile a class book of rhymes for everyone to read and enjoy.

Order of Lessons

You can make the charts in any order. Some teachers like to make all the short-**a** charts first, talk about the sound **a** makes in all these words, and then make charts for the other short vowels. Other teachers like to do all the different sounds for **a** and then move on to the other vowels. If you are using a basal reader or curriculum guide that specifies an order in which the vowel sounds will be taught and tested, let that order determine the order in which you make charts for *Reading/Writing Rhymes*.

Just as for *Using Words You Know*, use a rhyming dictionary, such as *Scholastic's Rhyming Dictionary* by Sue Young (Scholastic, 1994), as a source for the rhyming words. Pick the patterns that have the most rhyming examples. Some patterns will generate some "bad words." You can choose not to distribute the beginning letters that would make these words, or tell children that there are some words that could be made which "we never use in school" so you won't include them. (You don't need anyone to tell you what they are!)

Suggested Short Vowel Patterns for Reading/Writing Rhymes

For the short vowels, these are the most common rhyming patterns:

a:	ack	ad	am	ap	ash	at	an	and
e:	ed	et	est	ell	en			
i:	ick	id	ip	ill	it	in		
o:	op	ot	ock	ob				
u:	uck	ug	ump	unk	ut	unch		

The next most common vowel sounds are sometimes called the "long" sounds. Some children find it easier to figure out these long vowel words because they can actually hear the vowel "saying its name." Again, don't confuse children by placing too much emphasis on the terminology or the rules. Rather, have them notice the patterns.

The easiest and most consistent long vowel spelling for **a** is the **a-y** pattern, so begin with that one, using the same procedure of handing out all 50 beginning letter cards. Invite children who have letters they think will make real words to come up, place their cards next to the **ay**, say the words, and use the words in sentences. When they have not noticed that their letters will make a word, clue them by saying something like, "I think the person who has the **br** could come up here and spell the word that is the sound a donkey makes."

Just as for short vowels, finish by adding longer **ay** words that rhyme, along with any common rhyming words with a different spelling pattern. The children are always amazed at how many wonderful rhyming words there are on the **ay** chart and eagerly write lots of silly rhymes.

_ay	
day	today
say	Monday
way	Tuesday
play	Wednesday
lay	Thursday
bay	Friday
hay	Saturday
may	Sunday
May	birthday
stay	away
stray	highway
clay	x-ray
gray	yesterday
pray	holiday
pay	faraway
way	subway
tray	*sleigh
Ray	*weigh
ray	*hey
sway	*they
slay	*ballet
bray	*croquet
spray	

The second most common way of spelling the long-**a** vowel sound is to have an **a**, followed by a consonant, and then a "silent" **e**. A good way to introduce this is with the **ake** pattern, because it has many appealing rhyming words. The other common combination for the long-**a** sound is **a-i**.

Many rhyming words can be spelled with **a-i** or **a-(consonant)-e**. The fact that there are two common patterns is not a problem when reading. Students quickly learn that both **a-i** and **a-(consonant)-e** often have the long **a** sound. When a child is spelling a word, however, she has no way to know which one is the correct spelling, unless she recognizes it as a word she knows after writing it. This is why we often write a word, think, "That doesn't look right," and then try writing it with another pattern to see if that looks right.

When writing rhymes which have two common spelling patterns, the teacher should write both patterns on the same chart. Students come up and tell the words their beginning letters will make, and the teacher writes them with the correct pattern. In many cases, there are homophones, words that are spelled differently and have different meanings but the same pronunciation. The teacher writes both of these and talks about what each one means. Artistic teachers draw a little picture next to one of these so that students can tell them apart. Here is the chart for the **ail/ale** long vowel spelling pattern:

_ail / _ale	
sail	sale
tail	tale
trail	whale
snail	Dale
Gail	gale
hail	Yale
bail	stale
fail	scale
mail	male
frail	pale
pail	tattletale
wail	wholesale
rail	female
quail	
nail	
jail	
detail	
monorail	
toenail	
cottontail	

Here are the long vowel combinations that have the most examples for rhyming patterns:

a:	ake	ail/ale	ain/ane	aid/ade	ait/ate	
e:	eat/eet	eal/eel	ead/eed			
i:	ice	ide	ine	ite/ight		
o:	old	o/oe	ow	oke/oak	ote/oat	oan/one
u:	ute/oot					

All the common vowel patterns can be taught through *Reading/Writing Rhymes*. Always choose the patterns that will generate the most rhymes. When there is more than one common spelling for a rhyme, include both—or in some cases all three—spelling patterns. **Here are the other vowel sounds that are common enough to merit teaching:**

The R-Vowel Patterns:

ar	**ark**	**art**
are (care)/air	**ear (near)/ere/eer**	
ert/irt/urt	**irl/url**	**urn/ern/earn**
orn	**ort**	**ore/oar**

The special sounds of the vowel **a** when it is followed by **l**, **w**, or **u**:

aw	**all**	**awl**	**aul**

Some people consider the **ank, ang, ink,** and **ing** patterns to be long vowels and some people consider them to be short vowels. In many dialects, they are somewhere between these long and short sounds. In any case, they are common enough so that children should learn them:

ank	**ang**	**ink**	**ing**

O is the vowel with the most different sounds. *Reading/Writing Rhymes* Charts might be made for these:

ook	**ood**	**oom**	**ool**
oy	**oil**	**out**	**ow (how)**
ew/ue/oo (too)			

The letter **y** functions as a vowel in some words. Here are charts for its most common sounds:

−y

my	butterfly
by	deny
sky	defy
spy	reply
sly	rely
shy	qualify
why	satisfy
cry	multiply
dry	*good−bye
fry	
fly	
try	
sty	
pry	
*eye	
*die	
*tie	
*lie	
*pie	
*buy	
*guy	

−ary	−airy	−erry	−arry
Mary	airy	cherry	carry
scary	dairy	ferry	marry
Gary	hairy	Terry	tarry
Cary	fairy	merry	Harry
vary		raspberry	Larry
canary		strawberry	
January		*very	
February		*bury	
dictionary			
military			
necessary			
ordinary			
secretary			

Decoding and Spelling Variations

Decoding and spelling activities which occur in the 20-25 minutes of the Working with Words Block (following Word Wall every day) vary depending on the needs of children, the personality of the teacher, grade level, and time of year. If the teacher tries to make each of these activities as multilevel as possible, there is not as much variance for time of year and grade level as might be expected.

In early first grade, the teacher should spend a lot of time with phonemic awareness activities that help children learn to segment and blend words and to deal with the concept of rhyme. Teachers should continue to include some work with phonemic awareness throughout first grade and into second grade, because many children require lots of varied practice with this before they truly understand it.

Rounding Up the Rhymes

Rounding Up the Rhymes is an activity which can be used numerous times throughout the primary grades. The procedures are the same but the books from which the class is working, and the rhyming patterns, are different each time.

Making Words

Teachers should use fewer letters and only one vowel in early *Making Words* lessons. From the five letters **i**, **k**, **n**, **s**, and **t**, for example, the class might make the words **in**, **it**, **sit**, **kit**, **kin**, **skin**, **sink**, and **stink**. Even in these early lessons, students should sort for patterns and use sorted rhyming words to read and spell some transfer words.

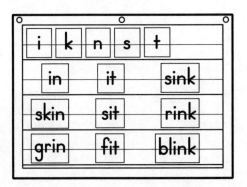

In the example lesson, the words were first sorted according to initial letters and then into rhyming words. These rhyming words were used to figure out how to decode **fit** and **grin** and how to spell **rink** and **blink**.

Guess the Covered Word

Teachers should only cover words with single initial consonants in the first *Guess the Covered Word* lessons, but soon include words that begin with letter combinations such as **s-h** and **b-r**. They should never completely move away from including some words with single consonants, however.

For the first lessons, only words at the ends of sentences are covered. Later, covered words occur anywhere in the sentence. Teachers can also do some lessons in which the covered words occur in paragraphs taken from stories or informational books.

Using Words You Know

Using Words You Know lessons can be used to teach any vowel patterns. They are perfect for second grade, are often used late in the year in first grade, and are fun and motivating for third graders who still haven't quite figured out "how you do it."

Reading/Writing Rhymes

Reading/Writing Rhymes is most effective in second and third grades. Teachers choose the patterns depending on which phonics and spelling principles their students need to learn or review.

MAKING THE WORKING WITH WORDS BLOCK MULTILEVEL

All of the activities in the Working with Words Block are inherently multilevel. Here is a description of how each activity benefits children of all abilities within a classroom:

Word Walls

Someone watching children doing the daily Word Wall practice might assume that they are all learning the same thing—how to spell words. What they are doing externally, however, may not reveal what they are processing internally.

Imagine that the five new words added to the wall one week were **come**, **where**, **they**, **boy**, and **friend**. During the daily Word Wall practice, the children who have already learned to read them are learning to spell them. Other children, however, who require lots of practice with words, are learning to read them. Still other children are learning to use these words to read and spell lots of words.

Rounding Up the Rhymes

While *Rounding Up the Rhymes*, some children are still developing their phonemic awareness as they decide which words rhyme and are learning that rhyming words usually—but not always—have the same spelling pattern. As they use the words rounded up to read and spell new words, children who need it are getting practice with beginning letter substitution. Children who already have well-developed phonemic awareness and beginning letter knowledge are practicing the important strategy of using known words to decode and spell unknown rhyming words.

Making Words

Making Words lessons are multilevel in a number of ways. Each lesson begins with short, easy words and progresses to some medium-size and big words. Every *Making Words* lesson ends with the teacher asking, "Has anyone figured out the word we can make if we use all our letters?" Figuring out the secret word which can be made from all the letters in the limited time available is a challenge to even the most advanced readers. *Making Words* includes even children with very limited literacy who enjoy manipulating the letters and making the words even if they don't get them completely made until the word is made in the pocket chart. Ending each lesson by sorting the words into patterns, and then using those patterns to read and spell some new words, helps children of all levels see how to use the patterns they see in words to read and spell other words.

Guess the Covered Word

Guess the Covered Word lessons provide review for beginning letter sounds for those who still need it. The most sophisticated readers are consolidating the important strategy of using meaning, all the beginning letters, and word length as clues to the identification of an unknown word.

Using Words You Know

Using Words You Know lessons provide children who still need it with lots of practice with rhyming words and with the idea that spelling pattern and rhyme are connected. Depending on what they already know, some children realize how words they know can help them decode, while other children realize how these words help them spell. To make the lesson a bit more multilevel at the upper end, include a few longer words that rhyme and help students see how their known words can help them spell the rhyming part of longer words.

Reading/Writing Rhymes

Reading/Writing Rhymes is perhaps the most multilevel activity. All beginning letters, including the common single consonants and the less-common, more-complex digraphs and blends, are reviewed each time the teacher distributes the onset cards. Phonemic awareness is developed as children say all the rhyming words and blend the vowel patterns with the beginning letters. Children whose word awareness is more sophisticated learn that there are often two spellings for the long vowel patterns and develop their visual checking sense as they see the rhyming words with the different patterns written on the same chart. They also learn the correct spelling for many of the common homophones. The addition of some longer rhyming words helps them learn how to decode and spell longer words and allows them to write more interesting rhymes.

Kids' Comments about Working with Words:

"I like doing Word Wall because I like to learn how to spell new words."

"I like Word Wall because I like clapping and spelling the words in the air. Doing word patterns is fun, too."

"I like *Making Words* because I like going up and spelling words."

"I like Working with Words because you learn a lot."

"I like *Making Words* because it helps you learn words."

"I like *Reading/Writing Rhymes* because you get to write silly rhymes."

"I like *Guess the Covered Word* because it is fun to play."

The pages at the end of this chapter provide a summary and review of information on the Working with Words Block. There is an example of how one week in this block might look. Finally, there is a checklist many teachers use when they begin implementing this framework.

SUMMARY OF THE
WORKING WITH WORDS BLOCK

The purpose of this block is to ensure that children read, spell, and use high-frequency words correctly, and that they learn the patterns necessary for decoding and spelling.

Total Time: 30 minutes (Pacing is critical!)

10 min.

Segment One: Word Wall

The teacher introduces five Word Wall words each week by having students do the following:

- See the words.
- Say the words.
- Chant the words (snap, clap, stomp, cheer, etc.).
- Write the words and check them together with the teacher.
- Trace around the words and check them together with the teacher.
- Do *On-the-Back* activities involving the words.

On days of the week when new Word Wall words are not the focus, the teacher reviews previous Word Wall words. When children can cheer for, write, and check five words in less than ten minutes, the remaining minutes are used for an *On-the-Back* activity.

20 min.

Segment Two: Decoding/Spelling Activity

The teacher guides activities to help children learn spelling patterns. Activities may include any of the following:

- **Making Words**, in which children manipulate letters of the alphabet to construct words, sort words into patterns, and use the sorted rhyming words to spell and read new words.
- **Guess the Covered Word**, which helps students learn to cross check meaning and letter-sound relationships.
- **Using Words You Know**, in which children learn how the words they already know can help them read and spell lots of other words.
- **Rounding Up the Rhymes**, which emphasizes spelling and rhyming patterns.
- **Reading/Writing Rhymes**, in which students use rhyming words to write and read some silly rhymes.
- Other activities that help children learn and use patterns to decode and spell words. (Cunningham, 1995)

A Typical Week in the Working with Words Block

Monday

Segment 1: Word Wall

The teacher introduces five new words. As each word is shown, students say the word, chant it, write it, trace around the word, and check it with the teacher. When that is complete, the teacher leads the students in a quick *On-the-Back* activity in which they write these five words in alphabetical order.

Segment 2: Making Words

The teacher leads the children in a *Making Words* activity using the theme-connected word, **airplane**, as the secret word. The activity leads them through making 14 words:

in	ran	pine	learn	airplane
an	pan	line	alien	
	pin	lane	plane	
		plan		
		earn		

The class then sorts for the **an**, **in**, **ine**, **ane**, and **earn** rhyming patterns. They use these rhyming words to figure out how to read and spell the transfer words **spine**, **spin**, **crane**, and **clan**.

Tuesday

Segment 1: Word Wall

The teacher reviews the five new Word Wall words for the week. The students say, clap, chant, write, and trace around these five words. Then the teacher leads the students in an *On-the-Back* activity in which they practice how one of the new words, **right**, can help them spell five other words: **fight**, **light**, **might**, **bright**, and **fright**.

Segment 2: Making Words

The teacher leads the children in a *Making Words* activity using the theme-connected word, **transport**, as the secret word. The activity leads them through making 13 words:

art	tart	ports	parrot	parrots	transport
	part	sport			
	port	start			
		tarts			
		toast			
		roast			

Then they sort for plurals and for the **ort**, **art**, and **oast** rhyming patterns. They use these rhyming words to figure out how to read and spell the transfer words **boast**, **chart**, **coast**, and **short**.

Wednesday

Segment 1: Word Wall

The teacher reviews five Word Wall words and then does a *Be a Mind Reader* activity on the back.

Segment 2: Rounding Up the Rhymes

The teacher uses the Dr. Seuss book, *Oh the Places You Will Go* (Random House, 1990), from Monday's Self-Selected Reading Block read-aloud, in a *Rounding Up the Rhymes* activity. The class rereads the book and uses several pages to collect rhyming words for the activity, then uses the rhymes with the same spelling pattern to read and spell four new words.

Thursday

Segment 1: Word Wall

The teacher reviews five Word Wall words, especially a couple of words with which the students are having difficulty in their writing. She then leads them to see how the words **write** and **want** are spelled when endings are added as the students write **writer**, **writing**, **wants**, **wanted**, and **wanting** in their *On-the-Back* activity.

Segment 2: Guess the Covered Word

The teacher leads the class in a *Guess the Covered Word* activity. The sentences reinforce information the class has learned about travel and transportation throughout the week.

Friday

Segment 1: Word Wall

Five "starred" words are called out, cheered for, and written. On the back, students decide which of the words they wrote on the front—**phone**, **drink**, **car**, **quit**, **trip**—will help them spell **bone**, **think**, **scar**, **chip**, and **skit**.

Segment 2: Using Words You Know

The teacher leads the class in a *Using Words You Know* activity in which they use **best**, **hope**, and **reach** to read and spell rhyming words, including these:

<u>**rest**</u>	<u>**rope**</u>	<u>**peach**</u>
quest	slope	beach
vest	cope	bleach
chest	grope	preach
nest		

TEACHER'S CHECKLIST FOR THE WORKING WITH WORDS BLOCK

In preparing and presenting my lesson in this block, I have...

_____ 1. Added only words to the Word Wall which are used frequently in reading and writing at this grade, and which should be spelled and used correctly.

_____ 2. Provided a good written and spoken model of the correct spelling and pronunciation of each of the Word Wall words.

_____ 3. Found ways (other than the Word Wall) to display words other than high-frequency ones that students will want to use in their writing. I have meaningfully clustered them (colors, numbers, theme charts) for easy access.

_____ 4. Practiced Word Wall words by chanting and writing. Included *On-the-Back* activities that help students explore words and transfer their learning to other words.

_____ 5. Planned *Making Words* activities which include small words, bigger words, and a secret word; sorted for patterns; and transferred sorted rhymes and patterns to read and spell a few new words.

_____ 6. Briskly paced my *Making Words* lesson by not waiting for each child to correctly spell the given word before sending a student to the chart to share the correct spelling with the class. Then, I have encouraged all students to check and spell correctly.

_____ 7. Planned *Guess the Covered Word* activities using all the onsets and led children to see that guessing a word that just makes sense is not particularly helpful, but guessing a word that makes sense, has all the correct beginning letters, and is about the right length is a very helpful decoding strategy.

_____ 8. Planned *Rounding Up the Rhymes*, *Using Words You Know*, and *Reading/Writing Rhymes* activities so that students learned a variety of rhyming patterns and used these to read and spell words.

_____ 9. Made sure that other activities included in the Working with Words Block helped children learn patterns, stressed transfer to reading and spelling new words, and were multilevel.

ANY QUESTIONS???

For us, the most interesting—and unpredictable—part of any workshop begins when we ask for questions. Some questions are unique and make us think beyond what we know. Other questions are asked again and again—by teachers all over the country—as they begin to consider what implementing the Four-Blocks framework in their classrooms will mean. Here are some of the most commonly-asked questions, our quick answers, and our thoughtful answers.

Do all children need all four blocks?

"No, but all classrooms full of children do!"

There are some children who seem equally engaged and successful in each block. These children would probably learn to read no matter what approach was used. Other children have clearly observable preferences, and if you watch closely, you can almost see them "click in" during the block which matches their learning personality. We have watched hundreds of classrooms learn to read within the Four-Blocks framework; and **in every classroom, we can identify children who would not learn to read as well if any block was eliminated.**

What happens to children in Four-Blocks classrooms who would otherwise be in the bottom group?

"They do better than when we had them in the bottom group!"

While we use many grouping formats for our instruction, we don't have fixed reading groups. The children have no notion of being in a top, middle, or bottom group. First graders who come to school with little print experience but much eagerness to learn maintain that eagerness and their "I can do anything" attitude. Many of our inexperienced first graders become grade-level or better readers and writers.

When we used to put children in the bottom group, we were combining two types of learners: slow learners and inexperienced learners. When slow learners and inexperienced learners are combined in a bottom group, the pace is slowed and the opportunity to learn is limited. When inexperienced, but fast, learners are given multiple opportunities to read and write and don't become discouraged by low group placement, they make up for lost time.

The bottom group is usually the most diverse group. It is more difficult to meet the students' needs when we lump them into one group than when we use a variety of individual, partner, and small-group formats. We began with the theory that grouping children was not the best solution to the multiple entering levels of children. Our abstract idea has now been replaced with tangible, "real kid" readers and writers.

Do the children who would have been in the top group get enough reading on their level?

"There is never enough, but they get more than they did when we had them in the top group!"

Perhaps the most surprising thing we have learned came not from the children with the lowest entering levels, but from those children already reading when they came to first grade—the ones who would have been placed in the top group. In all honesty, we didn't expect our model to make things much better for these children. We just hoped that not being in a top group wouldn't hurt them. As year after year of IRI data indicated that these children consistently read at fourth-grade level or above, we realized that **the Four-Blocks framework is probably as important for the highest achievers in each class as it is for the lowest**.

When our children were in reading groups, the top group in any grade level was usually placed in material just a little above grade level, but this upwards modification was not enough to accelerate the achievement of the very best readers. In the Four-Blocks framework, children spend half their time in the Self-Selected Reading and Writing Blocks, in which there is no limit to the level on which they can read and write. When there is no limit on how fast they can learn, our best readers, year after year, astonish us. It is clear to us now that **being in reading groups was as limiting for those in the top half of the top group as it was for those in the bottom half of the bottom group**.

What do you do about worksheets?

"As little as possible!"

The number of worksheets completed during the Four-Blocks time is minimal. One reason for this is that we don't need worksheets to keep the children busy. Another reason is that how well children read directly correlates to the amount of time they spend reading and writing. Finally, worksheets are not a very good use of children's reading and writing time, particularly for children whose reading levels are above and below grade level. **In order for a worksheet to help children grow in reading, it must meet three criteria:**

- First, **the worksheet must require that the child read and/or write**. This may seem so obvious as not to need mentioning, but consider some of the worksheets children in primary grades are given. Imagine that, as part of an animals unit, children complete a dot-to-dot sheet, connecting the dots and then coloring the lion they created. Imagine that they cut out and paste on additional body parts to create a new animal! While these worksheets are theme-connected, they involve minimal—if any—reading and writing. The time spent in these activities cannot possibly move children forward in reading and writing.

- The second criterion is that, once you have a worksheet activity that requires children to read and write, **children must be able to successfully complete it at an 80-85 percent level**. For most struggling readers, the only way they could achieve that level of success would be if they got their answers on the way to the pencil sharpener!

- The third criterion is the one that makes worksheets an unproductive use of time for above-average readers. **Students must need practice in whatever strategy or skill the worksheet is intended to reinforce.** Most of the best readers in any classroom can complete a worksheet perfectly in under ten minutes. They—and their parents—are happy to see all the 100's and stickers they bring home, but if the strategy being practiced is one they can already do fluently and without thought, they haven't grown through the completion of that worksheet.

The problem with worksheets is that they are not multilevel. The struggling readers can't do them, and the high achievers don't need them. How children use every minute of their time correlates very highly with reading achievement. Worksheets are seldom worth the time they take to complete. **We do occasionally use some worksheet activities to practice important skills. We often partner children so that struggling readers can successfully complete worksheets. We use some worksheets to add to our assessment portfolios.** Overall, however, time spent doing worksheets is very minimal across our Four-Blocks instructional time.

Are daily oral language exercises a part of the Four Blocks?

"No!"

Some classrooms were doing commercially produced daily oral language exercises before implementing the Four Blocks, and some classrooms continue them along with the Four Blocks, but they are not a part of the Four Blocks framework. We teach the concepts contained in daily oral language activities in a variety of ways which transfer to children's reading and writing. We build oral language in our discussions prior to and following Guided Reading. We model conventions and standard speech patterns in the writing we do each day in the minilesson which begins the Writing Block, and we help children learn to edit their own writing for items contained on the Editor's Checklist. We spend a great deal of time and effort in increasing oral language abilities, but we do not do this in an isolated fashion, removed from reading and writing. Rather, we integrate oral language development with reading and writing so that children can easily transfer increased oral language facility to their own reading and writing. In no case would we substitute a daily oral language exercise for the minilesson at the beginning of the Writing Block.

How do you get it all done?

"By not trying to 'add it on' and still do everything else!"

The Four-Blocks Framework is a framework for organizing instruction; it is not added on to what the teacher is currently doing.

- The basal or the traditional "reading instruction" is done during the Guided Reading Block.

- Writing becomes part of the Writing Block and is done in the writer's workshop format.

- Grammar and language skills are taught during the Writing Block.

- Spelling and phonics are taught in the Working with Words Block.

- D.E.A.R. is incorporated in the Self-Selected Reading Block.

Many of the blocks are familiar to teachers. Making the blocks multilevel is sometimes new, but that is not an add-on.

How do you give grades?

"With fear and trepidation!"

As teachers think about implementing the Four-Blocks in their classrooms, this is often the question that worries them most. We do not have a totally satisfactory answer to the question of how to grade, because the concept of giving grades—at least in primary grades—is not a realistic one. The notion of grades is that children all begin at the same place, and that those who work hard will get their just reward, and those who don't will be punished with bad grades. In early grades, however, this is not how things work. **Children come to us on all different levels and if we grade them by comparing everyone to everyone else, the struggling readers will fail—not because they don't try, but because of where they started. The high achievers will get wonderful grades—again, not because they are working so hard, but because of where they started.**

Imagine that you had a race and there were five different starting lines, best runners on the line 20 yards from the end, next best runners 30 yards back, average runners at the 40 yard line, slow runners at the 50 yard line and children who can barely walk at the 60 yard line. You start the race at the same time and the first children to get to the finishing point get A's, next B's, Next C's, and so on, until the last children finally arrive to claim their F's. Who do you think will get there first almost every time? Who will arrive last, and after several tries probably won't arrive at the finish line at all because failure is the reward for their efforts?

It is ridiculous to think that, in a race, people who are not good runners would have to start way behind the best runners, but that is what we do in schools when we feel everyone must meet the same criteria (get to the same finishing line) to make the grading system "fair." When we give everyone the same worksheets and tests and then base our grades on this, accelerated children learn that they can get A's with very little effort; struggling readers learn that they can't "make the grade" no matter how hard they try, and they soon stop trying. Traditional grading systems do nothing to motivate our best or our worst readers.

Most teachers in Four-Blocks classrooms are required to give grades, and they do. In giving grades to children in Four-Blocks classrooms, teachers **try to have the grades reflect growth, and communicate to parents both the starting point and the growth**. Teachers indicate if a child is reading at, below, or above grade level and include comments about specific strategies on which the child is working. They "justify" grades with work samples—first draft writing, published pieces, tape-recorded readings, running records, written responses to things read during Guided Reading, logs of books read during Self-Selected Reading, and occasional worksheets.

The true purpose of grades and report cards is to inform children and their parents about how they are doing and the progress they are making. When teachers have to give letter grades, they accompany these with comments about reading level, effort and progress. Struggling children who put forth effort do not get failing grades. Achieving readers only get A's if they too are putting forth effort and showing not only that they began ahead, but that they are continuing to grow.

How do special education children fit into Four-Blocks classrooms?

"Better than they fit into more traditional classrooms!"

Classrooms in which the Four-Blocks framework has been implemented include children with a variety of special needs. In most school systems, all but the most severely handicapped children are included in regular classroom settings. Schools vary as to the amount and type of support children get from other teachers and paraprofessionals, but the classroom teacher is primarily responsible for their language arts instruction.

We work hard to coordinate the efforts of the classroom teacher and those of the special teacher:

- Often special teachers come into the classroom and do their instruction there rather than taking children into another room. When special teachers are coming, most classroom teachers schedule either Guided Reading or Writing at that time because those blocks are the two that benefit most from an extra "pair of hands."

- When children must leave to go to a special teacher, we try to coordinate the specific instruction that teacher will provide with our classroom Four Blocks instruction.

Teachers—both classroom teachers and special education teachers—who have taught in traditional, ability-grouped classrooms consistently tell us that the needs of special education children can be more easily met within the Four-Blocks framework.

How can assistants or volunteers help in the Four-Blocks classroom?

"Let us count the ways!"

During Guided Reading, some students may occasionally enjoy reading to or with a volunteer or assistant. We all have students who need some individual encouragement, some one-on-one time with an adult. These may be students of any achievement level. After the pre-reading lesson, when students are reading with partners, flexible groups with the teacher, and/or small groups, one child can read with the helper. Together, they can read for the same purpose set by the teacher for all students. The assistant or volunteer might also monitor the reading partners to keep them focused. If a teacher is using book innovations or summaries to supplement the supply of appropriate easier reading, the helper might copy the innovations made by the teacher and the class, and make them into booklets to be distributed for partner reading.

During the Self-Selected Reading Block, a helper might occasionally provide the opening read-aloud. Remember that this serves as an invitation for kids to read. The volunteer or assistant may need assistance in choosing an appropriate book for this and will certainly need to practice the text before reading to the children. The read-aloud must be motivational for children. While children read and the teacher conferences, the helper might go around and encourage individual children in their reading.

During the Writing Block, volunteers may circulate among the students offering encouragement that the teacher may not be free to do since the teacher is conferencing with individual children. The volunteer should ask individual students what they're writing, offer positive comments, and may ask some students to read their writing aloud to her. Helpers should not spell words for children, but should help them stretch words out or point out where in the room the needed word is displayed. Some helpers construct pre-made books into which the children will copy their final drafts for publication; the children's published work can then be displayed in the hall or in the classroom.

During the Working with Words Block, a volunteer or assistant might be asked to sit with a struggling student who needs some help keeping up with the fast-paced activities, such as *Making Words*. The helper should be instructed to help the child hear the sound of the words he is attempting to build and to help nudge the child in the right direction in removing and adding letters. In preparation for the Working with Words Block, a helper might make words for the Word Wall (at the direction of the teacher); construct packets of *Making Words* lessons, and/or sort and distribute the letters for *Making Words*.

Can you do ability grouping and the Four Blocks?

"We do not recommend it."

Not putting the children in fixed ability groups is one of the basic tenets of Four-Blocks instruction. There are many reasons for this. Children placed in the bottom group often perceive themselves as poor readers and act accordingly. The bottom group contains an inordinate number of children with attention/behavior problems, and it is difficult to keep them all focused and on task. Some children who would be placed in the bottom group are not slow learners, they just have had fewer opportunities to learn. When they are placed in the bottom group and the instruction is slowed, they then become slow learners. There are always differences in reading levels, and bottom-group instruction will tend to be geared either toward the highest end of the group or the lowest end—thus not meeting the needs of the other end. There is also a lot of range in the top group, and the instruction tends to be pegged just a little above grade level—thus not meeting the needs of the really superior readers. Doing lots of little guided reading groups will take all your time and energy. The Writing Block, Self-Selected Reading Block, and Working with Words Block are equally valid ways for children to learn to read, and they all require the teacher working with the children to be truly instructional approaches.

It is not difficult to make the Writing, Self-Selected Reading, and Working with Words Blocks multilevel (see descriptions of each). Guided Reading is the hardest block to make multilevel. We do some small group work during this block, and we include our struggling readers in guided reading groups more often than our accelerated readers. But, we change the students in this group regularly, and we always include some better readers for models. We also do some "after lunch bunch" easy reading groups in which we include the struggling readers, along with some better readers. Our struggling readers do not ever get the idea that they are "the bottom group."

Four-Blocks instruction is not ability grouped. Neither is it whole-class instruction in the grade-level books. We are very concerned with providing instructional-level reading for all children, but we make our instruction multilevel in a variety of ways in each block. We do not believe that Guided Reading is the only way to teach children to read. We teach children who struggle with Guided Reading, but who become wonderful readers because of the instruction the teacher provides during the Writing, Self-Selected Reading, and Working with Words Blocks.

Young children come to school with an "I can do anything" attitude. When children are placed in fixed-ability groups for all their literacy instruction, the bottom group of children have concluded that "Reading is one thing I can't do" by the end of first grade. Second-grade teachers tell us that the children in the bottom group come with an "attitude"—an attitude quite different from the attitude with which they entered school. Many children take longer to become literate, but our chances of teaching them are greatly increased if we can keep them thinking they can do it!

How do you do everything in the basal manual in a 30–40 minute Guided Reading Block?

"We don't!"

We are very choosy about which activities we do during Guided Reading, and we do some of the other activities during the other blocks. Because basals are designed to meet a wide spectrum of student and curricular needs, they offer far more activities than any one teacher should or could ever use. **Teachers must use their own professional judgement in selecting what is appropriate for their students.** For example:

- If it is good instruction, we use comprehension strategy lessons in the basal.

- We introduce some—but not all—of the vocabulary suggested, although we are much more apt to introduce it through picture walks and other book-connected activities than through charts.

- If there are sight-words, phonics, and spelling skills we deem worthwhile, we teach these during our Working with Words Block. Again, we teach these word skills in ways we consider more active and more multilevel than the activities suggested in most basal manuals.

- If there are writing skills—punctuation, paragraphs, etc.—included in the basal lessons, we work on these during the mini-lesson part of our Writing Block.

The Guided Reading part of the Four-Blocks framework is done with and without basal readers. Often, the adopted basal is used along with multiple copies of favorite children's books. **Whether we use basals or books during this block, we concentrate on comprehension strategies, development of vocabulary and word meaning, prior knowledge, and reading and rereading for fluency.** In Four-Blocks classrooms, we try to "do it all," but that does not include doing all the things in the basal manual.

Do you use the Four-Blocks framework in Kindergarten?

"No!"

While we do believe that kindergartners need many of the components of the Four-Blocks, we feel that a different way of organizing instruction is more appropriate for kindergartners. Most of our kindergarten literacy instruction is arranged around themes, and the reading and writing kindergartners do is connected to those themes.

In kindergarten, we include reading to children, with children (in a shared reading format), and by children. We include writing for children, with children (in a shared writing format), and by children. We also do lots of activities with words, letters, and sounds, with particular emphasis on developing phonemic awareness. The kindergarten program which we developed to build the foundation for literacy can be seen on the video, *Building Blocks* (Cunningham & Hall, 1996), and read about in *Month-By-Month Reading and Writing for Kindergarten* (Hall & Cunningham, 1997).

Do you use the Four Blocks in the intermediate grades?

"That depends!"

The Four-Blocks program was designed for instruction in the primary grades. **We believe that, until children have a strong, fluent third-grade reading and writing level, they need regular instruction in the four major approaches.** Once most of the children in a classroom are reading at the third grade level or above, we would include work in all the blocks, but we would not give them equal time and we would not necessarily do all four blocks every day. We might do longer Writing Blocks or Guided Reading sessions three days a week. As much as possible, we integrate Guided Reading and focused writing with each other and with the content areas of science and social studies. (The possibility of this kind of integrating is one reason we support self-contained intermediate classrooms.)

Words should get some attention in the intermediate grades—but not one-quarter of the time each day. Learning how to decode, spell, and gain meanings for polysyllabic words is the big word goal in the intermediate grades. Since most of these new big words occur in content areas, we would center our word instruction on content-area vocabulary.

We would still have a regular time each day for teacher read-aloud and Self-Selected Reading. In planning how much time to spend on reading and writing goals in primary grades, we divide our time up each day. For intermediate grades, we divide our time across an entire week of instruction. If, however, we have an entire classroom of intermediate-aged children, most of whom still read and write at first- and second-grade levels, we would use the Four-Blocks organizational framework.

The real question is not in what grade the children are, but on what level they are reading. For more information on how we would organize at intermediate grades, see *Classrooms that Work*, 2nd ed. (Cunningham & Allington, 1999). For specific Working with Words Block activities to do with intermediate-aged children who still struggle with reading and writing, see *Month-by-Month Phonics for Upper Grades: A Second Chance for Struggling Readers and Children Learning English* (Cunningham & Hall, 1998).

Is there a best order in which to do the Four Blocks?

"No!"

Once teachers decide on a schedule that works best for them, they usually do the same blocks at the same times each day, but we could show you any order you wanted to see. Teachers have a variety of reasons for scheduling certain blocks when they do. Some teachers do their favorite block first thing in the morning, to get the day off to a great start! Other teachers schedule their least favorite block first, to get it out of the way! (Yes, teachers have personalities, too, and like some blocks more than others!)

In some classrooms, a special teacher, assistant, or other helper comes for part of the day. Many teachers feel that Guided Reading and Writing are the two blocks that benefit most from having an extra adult in the classroom, and thus, schedule one or both of these when they have help coming.

We would like for any children who leave for special instruction not to miss one of the blocks unless we are absolutely certain they are receiving instruction in that approach while out of the classroom. If a child goes to Reading Recovery, for example, we know that child is getting the very best guided reading instruction, so we might schedule our classroom Guided Reading Block during that time. Another possibility is for the Reading Recovery teacher to alternate when children are taken so that they do not miss the same block every day.

Generally, we try to schedule our blocks when everyone is there. Sometimes this necessitates scheduling one or more blocks in the afternoon. This actually works out well for some children who are not "morning people."

Is FROG a part of the Four Blocks?

"No, but it is a wonderful addition."

FROG, Facilitating Reading for Optimum Growth (Hall, Prevette & Cunningham, 1994) was designed to provide daily small-group instruction to children in a Chapter 1 school. This school, Easton Elementary School in Winston-Salem, North Carolina, implemented the Four-Blocks framework. Because almost all the children in the school were at-risk for reading failure, they chose to support the Four Blocks with a small-group component.

For the FROG program, the role of existing personnel in the school is redefined to provide the number of teachers necessary to implement the program. Chapter 1 and other special teachers are organized into FROG teams which converge upon each classroom for 45 minutes each day. The students in each class are divided into small, heterogeneous groups which include one strong student, two or three average students, and one weak student. These groups receive daily intensive instruction with one of the FROG teachers or the classroom teacher. Each FROG session includes four 10-12 minute activities:

1. All children participate in Self-Selected Reading as part of their classroom instruction. **The FROG time begins with a discussion based on these self-selected books.** This discussion sometimes focuses on a particular literary element, such as author, character, plot, setting, mood, style, theme, or illustration. Children read and discuss parts of their self-selected books related to the literary element.

2. The second activity of FROG, **shared reading using predictable big books**, strengthens and supports the students' reading in the Guided Reading Block. Each FROG group spends an entire week with one big book, which they read and reread, and which is used to teach a variety of word, language, and comprehension strategies.

3. The third activity included in each FROG session is **a lesson to develop decoding and spelling strategies**. For this activity, teachers use a variety of activities including *Making Words*, *Rounding Up the Rhymes*, and *Guess the Covered Word*.

4. The final activity of FROG supports the classroom Writing Block. During classroom instruction, all children write on self-selected topics. During the FROG time, the predictable big book provides a model for teacher-directed writing instruction, allowing the children to make the reading-writing connection. **FROG ends each day with each child writing a focused sentence or two related to the big book.** The FROG teachers help their small group of children with ideas, language, spelling, and other mechanics as they write.

When the 45-minute FROG time ends, the FROG teachers "leap" to another classroom, and the classroom teacher continues instruction with the whole class in the Four Blocks. Reorganizing the special teachers into FROG teams provides the small-group support needed by many of the children in a Chapter 1 school to ensure their success in learning to read and write.

If you are using the Four-Blocks method, do you still need Reading Recovery or some other yearly intervention?

"Yes!"

No matter how comprehensive or how multilevel your program is, there will always be children who really struggle in the early stages of reading. These children benefit enormously from the tailored, one-to-one instruction they receive from a trained professional such as the Reading Recovery teacher. Over the years, many of the schools that have implemented the Four-Blocks framework have also implemented Reading Recovery programs. In those schools, the classroom teachers attest to the accelerated progress made by the Reading Recovery children. Reading Recovery teacher leaders who have programs in Four-Blocks schools (and in schools not using Four-Blocks) repeatedly tell us that they exit children more quickly when Reading Recovery tutoring is combined with a Four-Blocks classroom program.

How do you integrate instruction when you do four separate blocks each day?

"With lots of careful planning!"

While there is usually a separate time each day for each block, teachers do make connections from one block to another. **Many teachers take a theme approach to teaching**, and some teachers are better at integrating than others. These teachers often select books for Guided Reading which correlate with their theme. During the writing mini-lesson when the teacher models writing, she often (but not every day) writes something connected to the theme. Focused writing weeks also are generally theme-connected. Some of the books teachers read aloud at the beginning of Self-Selected Reading and some of the books from which children choose are theme connected.

Theme words are not put on the Word Wall; it is reserved for high-frequency words and words that represent high-frequency patterns. **Most teachers, however, have a theme board or chart in addition to the Word Wall.** This board changes with each theme and, in addition to pictures, includes theme-related words which children will need as they pursue that theme. Often the secret word in a *Making Words* lesson is theme-connected. Sometimes, the sentences or paragraphs used in *Guess the Covered Word* lessons relate to the theme.

In addition to theme connections, there are other connections across the blocks. We practice Word Wall words during the Working with Words Block, but we select them once they have been introduced in Guided Reading, or when we see many children misspelling them in first-draft writing. We make sure that the children know that when they are writing, they should spell words the best they can unless the word is on the Word Wall. Word Wall words must be spelled correctly!

Rounding Up the Rhymes occurs during the Working with Words Block, but the book from which we are rounding has usually been read by the children during Guided Reading or read aloud by the teacher to begin the Self-Selected Reading block. We often introduce vocabulary during Guided Reading through picture walks. While reading with small groups, we coach children on how to decode words using picture, context, and letter-sound clues.

In our mini-lesson at the beginning of each day's Writing Block, we model how we can find words we need on the Word Wall and how to stretch out words, listening for the sounds, to spell big words not available in the room. When we are helping children edit, we praise them for their good attempts at spelling and coach them to use things they are learning during the Working with Words Block.

There are lots of ways to connect Guided Reading and Writing. If you are reading about a trip, you can write in your mini-lesson about a trip. If you are reading a funny story, you can write a funny story! If you are reading fiction, you can write fiction. If you are reading nonfiction, you can write an informational article! During the focused writing weeks, the teacher often connects the writing to what she is reading during Guided Reading.

Most teachers who have organized within the Four-Blocks framework find that it is natural and easy to make connections across the blocks. By providing instruction in all four blocks, we provide children with many different ways to learn to read and write. Connections across the blocks help children build bridges between what they are learning.

How do you get teachers to organize using the Four-Blocks framework?

"We appeal to their common sense!"

Although widely criticized for not being willing to try anything new, **teachers will change when the new program has lots of familiar elements, is "do-able" within the time frame and materials they have, and results in observably better readers and writers.**

Teachers have individual differences, too! Most teachers like some blocks better than others. They continue teaching each block each day, however, because they see children for whom each block is critical and are convinced that if they left any block out, some children would not learn to read as well.

Teachers appreciate the fact that they can take this framework and put their own "stamp" on it. What is the same in all classrooms is that we give each block its allotted time each day, and we work to make each block as multilevel as possible. Beyond that, there is wide latitude for teachers to carry out the instruction in ways they and the children find most satisfying and effective. Teachers also like the fact that there aren't a lot of papers to correct, and they get to know their students better as they work with them individually during Self-Selected Reading and Writing. (See How Teachers Grow with the Model, on pages 194-198, for teachers' thoughts before, during, and after implementing the framework.)

How can teachers modify the Four Blocks to fit their own classrooms?

"In any way that is consistent with the basic tenets of the Four-Blocks framework."

The basic tenets of the Four Blocks are few and simple. Since children do not all learn in the same way, we divide our instructional time and energy into four fairly equal time blocks, each of which provides children with a different approach to learning to read and write. The most basic tenet of the Four-Blocks method is that children are given 30-40 minutes of teacher-directed instruction each day in Self-Selected Reading, Guided Reading, Writing, and Working with Words. The second crucial tenet is that teachers provide instruction within each block to make that block as multilevel as possible. During Self-Selected Reading, the teacher's role is to model reading enjoyment; expose children to a wide variety of story and informational text through teacher read-alouds; and to provide weekly one-on-one instruction, encouragement, and assessment during individual conferences. In Guided Reading, teachers build comprehension using a variety of different kinds of reading texts and a variety of whole-class, small group, partner, and individual formats. During writing, teachers model how to write, revise, and edit during the minilesson that begins each writing block. As the children write, teachers provide individual instruction by conferencing with children about their writing. During the Working with Words Block, teachers make sure that children are learning to read and spell high-frequency words by doing a Word Wall activity each day. Next, they do a multilevel activity designed to help children learn patterns they can use to decode and spell lots of other words. Children are not placed in fixed-level groups during any of the blocks, but neither is this "whole class" instruction.

Working within these basic tenets of equal time to the Four Blocks and a variety of non-ability grouped, multilevel formats, there are an infinite variety of activities and materials teachers devise to make this instructional framework as effective as possible for their classroom full of children.

Is there research to support the Four-Blocks framework?

"Yes!"

The Four-Blocks framework was first implemented in one first-grade classroom. In the decade since then, the framework has been implemented in thousands of primary classrooms throughout the country. Different schools and school districts have different ways of assessing how children are growing and evaluating the instructional program. To answer the above question, we will summarize results from two schools and two districts. (For more details, see Cunningham, Hall & Defee, 1998.)

Clemmons Elementary School in Clemmons, North Carolina

Clemmons Elementary School, the school in which the framework was originally implemented, is a large suburban school with a diverse student population. Some children come from homes surrounding the school and others are bused from the inner city. In any year, 20-25 percent of children qualify for free or reduced-priced lunches. Approximately 25-30 percent of the children are African-American, Hispanic, or Asian-Pacific Islanders. Since the program began, the student population has remained relatively stable, with approximately 10 percent of the children moving in and out each year. All classes are heterogeneously grouped and contain an average of 22 children.

Throughout the year, teachers conduct assessment by observing and conferencing with children, taking running records, and looking at writing samples. At the end of the year, children are given the Basic Reading Inventory (Johns, 1994) by an assessment team headed by the curriculum coordinator. Instructional levels are computed using standard procedures, and include measures of oral reading accuracy and comprehension as measured by responses to comprehension questions. Because the IRI is administered at the end of the year, an instructional level of first or second grade is considered grade level at the end of first grade, and an instructional level of second or third grade is considered grade level at the end of second grade.

Across eight years of Four-Blocks instruction, results have remained remarkably consistent:

- At the end of first grade, 58%-64% of the children read above grade level (third grade or above), 22%-28% read on grade level, and 10%-17% read below grade level (pre-primer or primer). On average, one child each year is unable to meet the instructional level criteria on the pre-primer passage.

- At the end of second grade, the number at grade level is 14%-25%. The number above grade level (fourth grade level or above) increases to 68%-76%. The number reading below grade level drops to 2%-9%. Standardized test data on these children collected in third, fourth, and fifth grades

Eight Years of Multimethod, Multilevel Instruction

Year 1 (Pilot Study in one first grade classroom) 1989-90

Year 2 (Grade 1)	1991		Year 3 (Grade 2)	1992	
Reading Levels:	No.	Percent	Reading Levels:	No.	Percent
Above (Gr. 3-6)	64	63%	Above (Gr. 4-6)	77	75%
At (Gr. 1,2)	28	27%	At (Gr. 2,3)	24	23%
Below (PP, P)	10	10%	Below (PP, P, Gr. 1)	2	2%
Year 3 (Grade 1)	1992		Year 4 (Grade 2)	1993	
Reading Levels:	No.	Percent	Reading Levels:	No.	Percent
Above (Gr. 3-6)	65	62%	Above (Gr. 4-6)	74	71%
At (Gr. 1,2)	26	25%	At (Gr. 2,3)	21	20%
Below (PP, P)	14	13%	Below (PP, P, Gr. 1)	9	9%
Year 4 (Grade 1)	1993		Year 5 (Grade 2)	1994	
Reading Levels:	No.	Percent	Reading Levels:	No.	Percent
Above (Gr. 3-6)	76	61%	Above (Gr. 4-6)	87	68%
At (Gr. 1,2)	28	22%	At (Gr. 2,3)	32	25%
Below (PP, P)	21	17%	Below (PP, P, Gr. 1)	9	7%
Year 5 (Grade 1)	1994		Year 6 (Grade 2)	1995	
Reading Levels:	No.	Percent	Reading Levels:	No.	Percent
Above (Gr. 3-6)	59	58%	Above (Gr. 4-6)	76	78%
At (Gr. 1,2)	25	25%	At (Gr. 2,3)	16	16%
Below (PP, P)	17	17%	Below (PP, P, Gr. 1)	6	6%
Year 6 (Grade 1)	1995		Year 7 (Grade 2)	1996	
Reading Levels:	No.	Percent	Reading Levels:	No.	Percent
Above (Gr. 3-6)	87	64%	Above (Gr. 4-6)	97	70%
At (Gr. 1,2)	29	22%	At (Gr. 2,3)	31	22%
Below (PP, P)	19	14%	Below (PP, P, Gr. 1)	10	8%
Year 7 (Grade 1)	1996		Year 8 (Grade 2)	1997	
Reading Levels:	No.	Percent	Reading Levels:	No.	Percent
Above (Gr. 3-6)	85	64%	Above (Gr. 4-6)	118	74%
At (Gr. 1,2)	32	24%	At (Gr. 2,3)	26	20%
Below (PP, P)	15	11%	Below (PP, P, Gr. 1)	8	6%

each year indicates that 90% of the children are in the top two quartiles. Most years, no children's scores fall in the bottom quartile.

Lexington One in Lexington, South Carolina

The original school in which the framework was implemented does not do standardized testing until the end of third grade. Other districts, however, do administer standardized reading tests in the primary grades, and one district devised an evaluation model, the results of which will be reported here.

Lexington One in Lexington, South Carolina, is a suburban southeastern school district with eight elementary schools, in which 25% of the children qualify for free or reduced-price lunch. During the 1995-96 school year, first-grade teachers in the district were given information about the Four-Blocks framework and allowed to choose whether or not they wanted to implement the framework in their classrooms. Approximately half of the teachers chose to implement the framework and were provided with several workshops, books, and collegial support throughout the year.

In January 1996, 100 first graders in classrooms using the Four-Blocks framework and 100 first graders in classrooms not using the framework were randomly selected and given the Word Recognition in Isolation and Word Recognition in Context sections of the Basic Reading Inventory (Johns, 1994). Adjusted means for both measures favored students in the Four-Blocks classrooms. For the Word Recognition in Context means, the differences were statistically significant. **Students in the Four-Blocks classrooms were on average reading at the beginning of second grade level. Students in the other first grades were on average reading at the first grade, second month, level.**

While these results were encouraging, district officials were concerned about lack of reliability on the IRI, and about teacher bias, fearing that the enthusiasm of the teachers who chose to implement the model may have created a Hawthorne effect. They then devised an experiment using cohort analysis and standardized test results. In May of 1996, all 557 first graders in Four-Blocks classrooms were administered the Metropolitan Achievement Test. Each child was matched with a first grader from the previous year (1994-95) based on scores on the CSAB (Cognitive Skills Assessment Battery), a test of readiness given each year during the first week of school. **The total reading mean score for the Four-Blocks first graders was significantly better** (.0001 level) than that of the previous year's matched students. In grade-equivalent terms, the average Four-Blocks first grader's total reading was 2.0 while that of the 1994-95 student was 1.6.

This district then analyzed the data by dividing both groups of students into thirds according to their CSAB scores. This analysis demonstrated that children of all ability levels profited from the multilevel Four-Blocks instruction. There was a 15-point difference in total reading scores for the lower third, a 23-point difference for the middle third, and a 28-point difference for the upper third. The district concluded that **organizing in this nonability grouped way had profited the strug-**

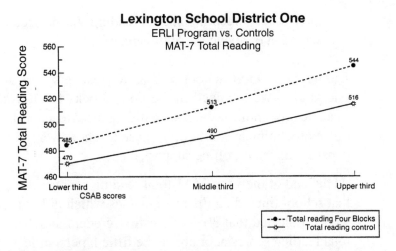

Lexington School District One
ERLI Program vs. Controls
MAT-7 Total Reading

gling students and had been even more successful for students who would traditionally have been placed in the top group.

Brockington Elementary School, South Carolina

During the same year, a nearby school adopted the Four-Blocks framework and mandated its use in all first- and second-grade classrooms. Brockington Elementary School in Florence School District Four in Timmonsville, South Carolina, is a small rural district in which 84% of students qualify for free or reduced-price lunch. Based on low achievement-test scores, the elementary school had been placed on the list of the state's lowest-performing schools and had tried a variety of approaches to improving reading and math test scores:

- During the 1991-92 school year, the school was mandated by a new superintendent to "teach the basics." A state-developed basic skills curriculum focused on "skill and drill" was implemented, along with a computer-lab basic skills remediation program for Chapter 1 students. End-of-the-year achievement test scores showed no improvement.

- During the 1992-93 school year, teachers took a yearlong graduate course on whole language. Again, the end-of-year test results failed to show improvement.

- During the 1993-94 school year, another new superintendent arrived. The district continued to emphasize whole language and teachers were trained in cooperative learning. This year's test scores showed some improvement at grades two and three, but none at grade one.

- During the 1994-95 school year, teachers were urged to continue to use whole language and cooperative learning, and they were also trained in the Learning Styles approach of Rita Dunn. It is hard to compare test scores for this year because the state changed from the Stanford Achievement Test to the Metropolitan Achievement Test, but scores were the worst they had ever been. In grade one, only 20% of the students scored at or above the fiftieth percentile on total reading. At the second grade level, only 9% scored at or above the 50th percentile.

During the 1995-96 school year, all ten teachers—six at first grade and four at second grade—were trained in the Four-Blocks framework. (It boggles the mind to imagine how enthusiastic and confident these teachers must have been to implement one more "miracle solution!") These teachers were given workshops/books, state-department/central office support, etc.

At the end of the year, MAT total reading scores for all first and second graders in that school (including the three classes which did not really implement the framework) indicated that 30% of the first graders and 38% of the second graders had total reading scores at or above the fiftieth percentile.

The data from this school system are, of course, open to interpretation. Since different children were tested in the 1994-95 group and we have no pretest data on these children, we cannot be sure that the huge jump in the number of children reading at or above grade level is due to the implementation of the Four-Blocks framework. Officials in this school district, having tried literally "almost everything" in the pre-

Brockington Elementary School
Timmonsville, South Carolina
Spring 1995, 1996, and 1997

MAT 7 Norm Referenced Tests
Comparison of Percentage of Students
Scoring at Each Quarter

Reading

Percentile	1995	1996	1997
76-100%	7	9	18
51-75%	12	20	28
26-50%	23	35	28
1-25%	58	36	26

Grade 1 Data

Reading

Percentile	1995	1996	1997
76-100%	1	14	11
51-75%	5	20	27
26-50%	25	40	38
1-25%	68	26	24

Grade 2 Data

MAT 7 Norm Referenced Tests
Percent At/Above the 50th National Percentile

Reading

Grade	1995	1996	1997
1	20	30	46
2	9	38	40
3	23	19	*33

* First year of implementation at grade 3, and first year with third grade students who had previously received Four-Blocks instruction.

Brockington Elementary School
Basic Skills Assessment Program
State Criterion-Referenced Test
Grade 3 with One Year of Implementation

	1996 % of Students Meeting Standard	1997 % of Students Meeting Standard
Reading	60.0	87.8
Math*	61.2	90.0

* A common phenomenon has been the rise in math scores consistent
with the increases in reading/language scores in Four-Blocks schools.

vious five years, are convinced, however, that the differences are real and attributable to the balanced, multilevel instruction which most of the 1995-96 first and second graders received on a daily basis.

Parkway School System in St. Louis, Missouri

Parkway School System is located outside St. Louis, Missouri. Some of their students, however, are bused from the city to achieve racial integration. This school system began the Four-Blocks model in two schools in the 1995-96 school year, expanding it to several other schools the next year.

The third year, they wanted to implement the framework in all of their schools. Before doing this, they looked at the students' fall and spring Gates McGinite Reading scores of two schools (one pilot and one control) to see if the framework had been effective. In the fall, students at both schools were scoring about the same on this test. There was no statistically significant difference between their scores. **In the spring, however, scores at the pilot school were clearly higher than the control school, and the difference was statistically significant. So, students at both schools started out at the same reading level, but the students at the pilot school were reading better than students at the control school by the end of the year.**

The results of a covariance analysis showed the pilot school still above that of the control school, and the difference was still statistically significant. So, even when you take into account the slightly better beginning scores, they still performed significantly better than the control students at the end of the year.

The next question they asked was, "Does this pattern hold true for students of different abilities?" They defined "average" scores as those that fall between the 34.0 and 65.0 NCE (twenty-third and seventy-sixth National Percentile Rank). They described "below average" as below the twenty-third percentile on the Gates and "above average" as above the seventy-sixth percentile on the Gates. At the pilot school, all three groups of readers showed significant improvement in their reading scores from fall to spring. At the control school, only the average readers demonstrated statistically significant change in their scores from fall to spring. The difference in improvement rates among below average and above average readers at the two schools was statistically significant. **This pattern of scores shows that all types of students performed better with the Four-Blocks framework.**

Warren Consolidated Schools in Warren, Michigan

Warren Consolidated Schools in Warren, Michigan, designed an experimental test of the Four-Blocks framework compared to a more traditional basal reader framework. Teachers who were using the system-adopted basal, but following the Four-Blocks literacy framework, were compared with teachers who used the same basal series and followed its components. Various data from the pilot and control groups were analyzed to determine whether the Four Blocks should be considered for implementation by all first-grade teachers. From 14 classrooms, 62 children were randomly selected for extensive testing. The following tests were administered throughout the year: alphabet recognition, words known, dictated sentences, an IRI, a spelling test, Botel Word Opposites, and writing samples. Surveys were filled out by the teachers and parents of the students involved in the study.

The test data collected indicated that, although the pilot group included more children who were boys, more on medication, and more who were bilingual, all the results on the individual tests for the Four-Blocks children surpassed those of the control group. The school system concluded that they would promote this framework within all first-grade classrooms in their district.

The Four-Blocks framework has not only been used to teach a wide variety of children to read, it has also been shown to produce better readers as measured in a number of different ways in a number of different school systems. Data from five different school systems in four different states suggests that combining instructional methods for a balanced approach results in better reading on a variety of measures. The results that are most impressive are those that show that all children improve their reading with this framework regardless of their entering literacy levels.

PROFESSIONAL REFERENCES CITED

PROFESSIONAL RESOURCES

The Art of Teaching Writing (2nd ed.) by L. M. Calkins (Heinemann, 1998).

Basic Reading Inventory (5th ed.) by J. L. Johns (Kendall Hunt, 1994).

Becoming a Nation of Readers by R. C. Anderson, E. H. Hiebert, J. A. Scott & I. A. G. Wilkinson (U.S. Department of Education, 1985).

Building Blocks: A Framework for Reading and Writing in Kindergartens That Work by P. M. Cunningham & D. P. Hall (Windward Productions, 1996).

Classrooms that Work by P. M. Cunningham & R. L. Allington (Addison Wesley Longman, 1999).

"Eliminating Ability Grouping and Reducing Failure in the Primary Grades" by D. P. Hall, C. Prevatte & P. M. Cunningham (in *No Quick Fix*, R. L. Allington & S. Walmsley, editors, Teachers College Press, 1995, pp. 137-158).

The Four Blocks: A Framework for Reading and Writing in Classrooms That Work by P. M. Cunningham & D. P. Hall (Windward Productions, 1996).

A Fresh Look at Writing by D. H. Graves (Heinemann, 1995).

Implementing the 4-Blocks Literacy Model by Cheryl Mahaffey Sigmon (Carson-Dellosa Publishing, 1997).

Individualizing Your Reading Program by J. Veatch (Putnam, 1959).

Invitations (2nd ed.) by R. Routman (Heinemann, 1995).

"KWL: A Teaching Model That Develops Active Reading of Expository Text" by D. Ogle (*The Reading Teacher*, Vol. 39, 1986, pp. 564-570).

"KWL Plus: A Strategy for Comprehension and Summarization" by E. Carr & D. Ogle (*Journal of Reading*, Vol. 30, 1987, pp. 626-631).

Making More Words by P. M. Cunningham & D. P. Hall (Good Apple, 1997).

Making Words by P. M. Cunningham & D. P. Hall (Good Apple, 1994).

Month-by-Month Phonics for First Grade by P. M. Cunningham & D. P. Hall (Carson-Dellosa Publishing, 1997).

Month-by-Month Phonics for Second Grade by D. P. Hall & P. M. Cunningham (Carson-Dellosa Publishing, 1998).

Month-by-Month Phonics for Third Grade by P. M. Cunningham & D. P. Hall (Carson-Dellosa Publishing, 1998).

Month-by-Month Phonics for Upper Grades by P. M. Cunningham & D. P. Hall (Carson-Dellosa Publishing, 1998).

Month-by-Month Reading and Writing for Kindergarten by D. P. Hall & P. M. Cunningham (Carson-Dellosa Publishing, 1997).

"Nonability Grouped, Multilevel Instruction: A Year in a First Grade Classroom" by P. M. Cunningham, D. P. Hall & M. Defee (*Reading Teacher*, Vol. 44, 1991, pp. 566-571).

"Nonability Grouped, Multilevel Instruction: Eight Years Later" by P. M. Cunningham, D. P. Hall & M. Defee (*Reading Teacher*, Vol. 51, 1998).

Phonics They Use: 2nd Edition by P. M. Cunningham (Addison Wesley Longman, 1995).

"Reading Aloud in Classrooms: From the Modal to a 'Model'" by J. Hoffman, N. L. Roser & J. Battle (*The Reading Teacher*, Vol. 46, 1993, pp. 496-505).

CHILDREN'S BOOKS CITED

Animal Tracks by Arthur Dorros (Scholastic, 1991).

Brown Bear, Brown Bear, What Do You See? by Bill Martin, Jr. (Holt, Rinehart, Winston, 1967).

Cats by Gail Gibbons (Holiday House, 1998).

Hattie and the Fox by Mem Fox (Simon and Schuster, 1968).

I Went Walking by Sue Williams (Harcourt Brace, 1990).

Ira Sleeps Over by Bernard Waber (Houghton Mifflin Co., 1979)

The Lion and the Mouse retold by Cheyenne Cisco (William H. Sadler, 1997).

Make Way for Ducklings by Robert McCoskey (Viking, 1976).

Moonbear's Books by Frank Asch (Simon & Schuster, 1993).

The Mouse and the Motorcycle by Beverly Cleary (Mass Market Paperback, 1996).

Oh, the Places You Will Go! by Dr. Seuss (Random House, 1990).

Sea Turtles by Gail Gibbons (Holiday House, 1998).

Sharks by Gail Gibbons (Holiday House, 1993).

Strega Nona by Tomie de Paola (Aladdin Paperbacks, 1988).

Swimmy by Leo Lionni (Knopf Children's Paperbacks, 1992).

Three Cheers for Tacky by Helen Lester (Houghton Mifflin, 1994).

Wolves by Gail Gibbons (Holiday House, 1995).

Wonderful Worms by Linda Glaser (Milbrook Press, 1992).

What Do Teachers Say?

HOW TEACHERS GROW WITH THE MODEL
(AN EVOLUTION OF TEACHERS' THOUGHTS BEFORE, DURING, AND AFTER IMPLEMENTATION OF FOUR-BLOCKS)

Interviews with teachers who have had at least one year of experience with the model revealed growth through the following statements:

Prior to the Model

"I was convinced that there was no way to meet the needs of all kids in truly hetero-geneous classes. I wanted it to work, but it just didn't."

"I was frustrated. I had to resort to worksheets to keep some kids busy so I could work with groups. I was desperate to find something that made me feel comfortable and confident."

"Like a lot of other teachers, I knew intuitively that one approach to reading was never going to reach all of the children in my class. Before being introduced to Four Blocks, though, I would have thought it totally mind-boggling to blend all of the major approaches to teaching reading to all kids at the same time! I would never have dreamed it possible!"

"I considered myself a pretty good teacher, but I was working *sooo* hard—only to get mediocre results. I really felt like I was doing the best job I could possibly do. My kids' parents just weren't doing what they needed to do. You know...pass the buck!"

Introduction of the Four-Blocks Model

"I was skeptical. So many new methods and theories have been thrown at teachers. All I could think was... 'Here we go again!'"

"My first impression of the model was that it made so much sense! At the same time, though, it sounded almost too easy to get the results that I heard others were getting."

"Learning about Four Blocks was not just about finding a new way to teach. We learned a lot about how children learn and specifically about how kids learn to read. The training was beneficial whether or not the model was adopted."

"I was apprehensive about getting started but enthusiastic at the same time."

Preparing for the Program

"The model requires an investment of time before you try to implement it. The materials aren't expensive, mostly just regular classroom and office materials. Most of the items help you get the Blocks—and your classroom—organized."

"I was still skeptical, but I was willing to give something new a try."

"Getting ready for my first Four-Blocks year was the beginning of my understanding of the advantage of teamwork. The preparation was fun and much easier when working with a group of other teachers."

"To me, making the materials to get started was fun!"

"Deciding how to get started was a hard decision for us. Should we start all Four Blocks at once or should we go one-by-one? Not all of us made the decision to start the same way. I think it depends on how much change you can tolerate. Some people fear change and need to start gradually. I finally decided I would try all four to a lesser degree and work on refining them."

Getting Started—The First Month

"Some of us were brave enough to get all four blocks up and going from the beginning. Some of the teachers at my school started with one block and kept adding one when they felt they could manage it. However we chose to get started, we all had to support each other. I can't say it was easy, but in retrospect it surely was worth it!"

"The first- and second-grade teachers at my school met regularly to discuss sections of *Classrooms That Work* and *Phonics They Use* to validate what we were doing and to continue to add new activities appropriately."

"Even in the first month, I could tell that my year was going to be a good one. Somehow through my initial training I had gained a clearer purpose and clearer goals for my teaching."

"I spent a great deal of time teaching kids the class routines—and there are a lot of routines with this model. I worried that I was neglecting real instruction."

"Teachers in my school who like quiet classrooms were struggling a bit. They had to learn to relinquish their position as sage on the stage. We talked a lot about the difference between noise from a lack of focus or control and noise from healthy interaction."

"We all began to see how the model was more student centered than we were used to."

"I had to work hard on my transitions from block to block. I didn't want my instruction to seem fragmented."

At Three Months

"I worried that I was shortchanging my top students, but they didn't seem bored at all. They were just as engaged as everyone else. I figured I'd just be patient for now."

"My toughest task was to stay focused on comprehension skills during the Guided Reading Block. I kept wanting to teach all of my skills during that time, just like I used to."

"It was hard not to layer the new methods on top of the methods I used prior to learning about the Four Blocks. I kept trying to add a safety net that really wasn't necessary."

"Pacing the blocks was very difficult for me. I had to buy a timer to help me."

"I set a goal to work harder on getting the students' works published more often."

"Luckily I had a great deal of support from my principal, a consultant, and other teachers. I had lots of questions and needed confirmation about my implementation."

"The kids knew the Four-Blocks routine well. They all seemed to have favorite activities."

"The children really were taking ownership into their literacy development with this model. For whatever reasons, they were more tolerant of individual differences than I had ever witnessed them being before. They knew that some kids were slower than others, and they really pitched in to help each other."

"I began to realize how hard I would have to teach with this model, began to worry that I wouldn't be able to sustain the energy level! The effects of the model, though, continued to energize me."

"I had never realized how much I was assigning to kids instead of actually teaching. It was especially apparent in the area of writing. Before, I was just assigning writing prompts and tasks. With Four Blocks, I was modeling for them daily and focusing on something that would help them to get better."

At the First Semester's End

"I had been trying to stick to the real basic activities in my block time through the first semester. I finally felt comfortable enough to add some new activities."

"In January, there was a definite, measurable difference in how my Four-Blocks class was outperforming any class I'd ever had before."

"Every child in my class saw him- or herself as a reader and a writer. That kind of confidence goes a long, long way!"

"I was finally convinced that I was truly meeting the needs of all the kids in my class—high achievers, low-achievers, and the average learners. Everyone was growing!"

"The teachers in my school who were trying the model were convinced it was working. We felt, though, that we were all a long way from feeling like we knew all that there was to know about the model. We were begging our principal and district for more training, especially to help us vary activities within the blocks. We still had lots of questions."

At the First Year's End

"What a year! I had a class of the best readers and writers I'd ever had before! Was it a coincidence? No way!"

"My first Four-Blocks year was a turning point for me professionally. I would never go back to the way I was teaching before."

"The teachers at my grade level were truly amazed that we had all been successful. The model was good for our kids and for us. It didn't seem to matter whether we were a first-year teacher or close to retirement, whether we were young or old, whether we considered ourselves traditional or progressive—we all had been successful with the model. Also, as far as the students, it didn't matter whether they were special needs kids, whether they were the 'gifted and talented,' whether they were from affluent or impoverished families—the model served them equally well. To say the least, our faculty was pleased!"

"I'm ready for another year!"

REPRODUCIBLES

The following pages are reproducible to use for

- **Parent Brochure about the Four-Blocks Method**
- **Bookmarks for students to use during reading activities**
- ***Making Words* homework sheet**

PARENT BROCHURE

As a teacher implements the Four-Blocks methods of teaching, it may be helpful to notify the children's parents. A reproducible brochure for the parents is found on pages 201-202. The brochure includes some general information about the Four-Blocks method, provides an overview of the types of activities in which the students will be involved, and contains ideas on how parents can help their children to become readers and writers.

The tri-fold brochure is two-sided. Use a utility knife or scissors to remove the page, photocopy, fold in thirds, and send out to parents.

BOOKMARKS

A classroom set of bookmarks can be reproduced on colorful paper and laminated. Use the reproducible bookmarks found on pages 203-205, or create your own bookmarks. Students can add their own designs to the bookmarks to use during the Self-Selected Reading Block. After the design is completed, the teacher can laminate the personalized bookmarks for greater durability. During their independent reading time, students can mark the place of a literary element or of something they want to discuss with the teacher during conference time. Teachers can instruct students to mark items that fit with a particular skill that is being studied, or let the students choose what they wish to mark and discuss during the conference time.

MAKING WORDS HOMEWORK SHEET

Use the reproducible worksheet found on page 206 when doing the *Making Words* activity with your students. See page 146 for complete instructions on using the homework sheet.

How You Can Help Your Child

- Talk about books with your child. Ask what he's read in school. Look for books to come home with him, and read *to* him, read *with* him, or simply *listen* as he reads. (The teacher will let you know which way is appropriate for your child.)

- Share often something that you're reading with your child—books, newspapers, recipes, magazines, etc.—to let her know that you value reading. Do the same with writing. When you write a note or letter, share it and talk about it with your child. Seeing their parents as readers and writers really makes an impression on children.

- Get a library card for your child at the public library, if possible, and visit on a regular basis.

- Consider giving your child a choice at bedtime: "Would you like for me to turn out the light, or would you like to read a book for 10 minutes?"

- Keep reading and writing materials available for your child.

- Read aloud to your child, even after he or she learns to read. Reading aloud should continue at least through elementary school.

- Try to attend school events, such as Open House and conferences with your child's teacher. We want to be partners in your child's education.

Did You Know...

Research supports that the single most important activity for building knowledge required for eventual success in reading is reading aloud to children.

Cited from Becoming a Nation of Readers

How Your Child Will Succeed at Reading and Writing This Year

Our school believes that children who are good readers and writers will be better, happier students and citizens. We have made a commitment to do all that we can to ensure that all of our students will be good readers and writers. Because our school recognizes that all children learn differently, we know that we must find ways to reach children no matter what their strengths and weaknesses might be. Our teachers are using a method of instruction called the Four-Blocks Model, and we want to tell you about it. We also want to ask that you play an important part in helping us with the development of your child as a reader and writer.

There are four basic ways that students have always learned to read. Usually, a school or teacher would choose one of those methods in hopes of reaching most of the students. The Four-Blocks Model, however, allows us to teach all students by teaching all four methods every day.

The Four-Blocks method has proven to be quite effective for the schools that implement it, and our teachers have worked hard to learn to use this method. We have four blocks of time devoted to language during the day. In this pamphlet, we have described what you might expect to see in the classroom during each block of language arts time. We invite you to come and visit to see how your child is learning and growing.

GUIDED READING BLOCK

During this block of time, we focus on reading comprehension skills—those strategies that help readers make sense out of the print on the page. We also work on our reading fluency—the smoothness with which we read text. The teacher will direct a lesson about a particular story or text with all of the students. Afterwards, our students will practice reading in pairs or small groups. Then, the teacher will again work with the whole group of students to discuss what they have learned. Students will get a great deal of support from their teacher, from their classmates, and will work toward becoming independent readers.

WRITING BLOCK

During this block, students will learn to think about and use their knowledge of phonics to write compositions. Along with applying phonics, they will have an opportunity to practice penmanship, to learn about the writing process, grammar, and the mechanics of good writing. Every day, the teacher will write her own composition for the students and will use it to teach a lesson about writing. Then, all students will write their own story or composition, using their best guesses about spelling. On certain days, the students will work individually with the teacher to learn to correct their errors, and they will publish their work as a book to be enjoyed by other classmates. At the end of the writing time each day, a few students will share their work with the class. It's truly surprising what an impact this block has on reading! Sometimes, the first text a child learns to read is his own.

SELF-SELECTED READING BLOCK

During this block, students will have an opportunity to see themselves as readers and will build their fluency, the ability to read smoothly. The block will begin with the teacher reading aloud an enjoyable story or text to the students. Then, each student will select a book from the book basket nearby to read independently for an extended amount of time, usually no more than twenty minutes. During this time, the teacher will have individual conferences with designated students. Together, they will discuss the book, and the teacher will be able to evaluate the student's growth in reading. At the end of the block, several students will share what they read and whether they liked the book, much like the way adults share information with their friends about the books they're reading.

WORKING WITH WORDS BLOCK

This block allows students to explore words, word families (patterns), spelling, and phonics, and to see how they can use what they learn about words in their reading and writing.

This block begins daily by studying words from the Word Wall. These words will be displayed on our wall all year for students to use as a resource. They are high-frequency words—grade-level words used frequently in reading and writing—that we expect students to spell correctly in their writing. We will use movements, such as clapping, snapping, and cheering, to learn to spell the words. We have a number of other activities to interest children during this word exploration time.

I want to try this in my own writing

Here is the main character!

Here is what the story is all about -- the theme.

Here is the solution.

Here is when and where the story takes place -- the setting.

Here is the problem in this story.

Reserved!

This book is waiting for _____ to return.

MY FAVORITE PART OF THE BOOK

A New Discovery!

THIS IS NEAT!!

I didn't understand this!